LOST ATE MY LIFE

The Inside Story of a Fandom Like No Other

Foreword by Lost Supervising Producer Javier Grillo-Marxuach

LOST
ATE MY LIFE

MEGA LOTTO JACKPOT

Your numbers are
4, 8, 15,

VODKA

The Inside Story of a Fandom Like No Other

by Jon "DocArzt" Lachonis & Amy "hijinx" Johnston

Published by ECW PRESS
2120 Queen Street East, Suite 200
Toronto, Ontario, Canada M4E 1E2
416.694.3348 / info@ecwpress.com

LIBRARY AND ARCHIVES OF CANADA CATALOGUING IN PUBLICATION

Lachonis, Jon
Lost ate my life : the inside story of a fandom like no other /
Jon Lachonis and Amy J. Johnston.

ISBN 978-1-55022-847-2

1. Lost (Television program) 2. Fans (Persons) 1. Johnston, Amy J.
11. Title.

PN1992.77.L67L32 2008   791.45'72   C2008-902429-X

Acquisitions editor: Nikki Stafford
Managing editor: Crissy Boylan
Cover Design: Grant Gould
Text Design and Typesetting: Melissa Kaita
Editor: Jen Hale
Printing: Transcontinental

PRINTED AND BOUND IN CANADA

ECW PRESS
ecwpress.com

DEDICATED TO *LOST* LABS

In Memory of Save the Humans, Oceanic_Lisa and Joe C.

Lost, but not forgotten

CONTENTS

ACKNOWLEDGMENTS

To Damon Lindelof and Carlton Cuse — for recognizing the value of communicating with the fans, thus making this book a reality rather than a work of fiction. To the Nomad — your continued participation on The Fuselage has been nothing short of fantastic. You have earned every bit of our loyalty.

To Javier Grillo-Marxuach — your brilliance as a writer is only surpassed by your devotion as a friend. When asked to write the foreword, you didn't even hesitate before agreeing to do it. As crazy as your own life has been, you still found the time to support, mentor and be a sounding board. Te debo.

To J.J. Abrams — for always giving us something amazing to watch, whether it be on the television or the movie screen. You and Bryan have filled Bad Robot with some of the nicest and most brilliant people on the planet. We look forward to being entertained for decades to come. Also to Katie McGrath — the sweetest woman on the face of the earth.

To William Mapother — for agreeing to be interviewed and for being so much fun to talk to, whether it be about *Lost* or Notre Dame.

To Grant Gould — for turning out a great cover that really represents the beautiful chaos of *Lost*, and this book.

To our editor Nikki Stafford — thanks for the handholding through all of this. Your patience and support of the n00bs exceeded that of mere mortals — we really cannot thank you enough. And thanks to Crissy, Simon and everyone else at ECW Press for helping us make this book what we always dreamed it would be.

hijinx's Acknowledgments

To Bryan Burk — there are not sufficient words to fully convey the depth of my gratitude. You are undeniably one of the most genuine people I have ever met, and your work ethic is staggering to behold. My participation in this book would *not* have happened without your blessing. Your support of me has been overwhelming and I can only hope you are pleased by the end result.

To Gregg Nations — you told me I should write a book and here it is. You planted the seed that sprouted this idea and have remained one of my biggest cheerleaders throughout this whole process. Thank you for your support, your friendship and your dedication to the show and its fans.

To Rick Orci — for listening to my rants, making me laugh, talking me off the ledge and keeping me sane (and humble). You understand my insanity better than even I do sometimes, and I value your friendship more than you'll ever know.

To Athena Wickham — for accepting me and trusting me from day one. But most of all, for caring about me more as a friend than as a fan. You make the impossible . . . possible. You are nothing short of amazing and I feel blessed to have you in my life.

To Dave Baronoff aka SCF — I am humbled by your unwavering belief in me and my capabilities. Thank you for making me feel way more important than I actually am, and for trying to protect me when things get too crazy in my world. I am incredibly lucky to be able to call you my friend. I have rarely encountered someone with a heart as big as yours.

ACKNOWLEDGMENTS

To Noreen O'Toole and Samantha Thomas — for keeping me up to speed on *Lost* Labs. You both have beautiful souls and light up any room you are in with your 1,000-watt smiles. I value your trust and your friendship.

To the Usual Suspects and the Mongers — for four years of love and support through laughter, BOARS and brain 'splodey. You guys rock so hard.

To the Posse aka Angela, Kelley, Tracie and Em — my first online friends and lifetime sisters. NBLFY.

To Dino, Russ and Milo, founders of the Divide Social Club — thank you for making a place that is accessible to anyone who wants to be a part of something bigger than themselves. I have a worldwide family because of your enormous hearts and boundless generosity. To my DSC family — for love, support, friendship and lots of laughs at any hour of the day, in any time zone. You guys are all SKA. DSC4Life.

To my co-writer Jon Lachonis — thanks for inviting me to embark on this journey with you, and for respecting *Lost* — the show, its creators and its fans.

To Andy Floyd aka Speaker aka Yang — for being the one person who totally gets every *squee* as well as every fear, every OMGWTF as well as every burden of being an "insider fan."

To Denise Yoder aka q — my best friend. Wherever this path takes me, I know you'll come with — CBA, but so much more than that to me. LYLAS.

To Jason Ward — for supremely awesome legal advice and guidance, and for asking me the most ridiculous questions about *Lost* just to get a rise out of me.

To Adam and Teresa Dahlgren — for your friendship and for opening your home to my kids and husband whenever I needed a quiet weekend to get some writing done.

To my parents, Joe and Carlene — for your support financially, emotionally and spiritually throughout this crazy journey. To my brother Ward — for being unfailingly honest with me, where others fear to tread. I hope I make you as proud of me as I am of you.

To my kids, Naomi and Matt — I do it all for you guys. I hope I make you proud.

And finally, to my husband Frank — thank you for loving me and supporting me, even when you don't share my obsessions. You bring me back to center whenever I get off track. I could *never* have done this without you.

DocArzt's Acknowledgments

Everyone in the *Lost* scene, Ben Sledge, Andy (DarkUFO), Andre and so on. It's the myriad viewpoints that make the scene what it is.

My co-writer Amy J. Johnston — for being much more than a co-writer; a motivator, a Fannie kicker and occasionally a psychologist.

Kevin Falls — for always being there with the aggressive "go for it" attitude.

Erin Felentzer and Jeff Fordis of ABC — for muddling through what is surely a sub-par level of professionalism on my behalf when it came to arranging interviews and show access for me over the years.

John Klyza — for all of the encouragement from across the pond.

Tom Ragg — for being a stream of constant positive energy.

Ed Kos — for taking the time out to show me and the family "the Island" as well as enriching our appreciation of Hawaii's history and agriculture.

Lost Virtual Tours — for filling in some of the nooks and crannies and taking me to some of *Lost*'s more extreme locations.

Lostpedia — for creating the best braindump for the *Lost* community.

Jeff Jensen — for always being accessible — especially in some tough times — and being a sort of personal trainer when it comes to dealing with the 'wood.

Michael Ausiello — for stuff we can't talk about without incriminating ourselves.

Jen Godwinn — for being Jen Godwinn, a person with better things to do than help me — but helps me anyways.

ACKNOWLEDGMENTS

ErasedSlate, Koobie, Adam, Tapdawg, WLN, Jopinionated, Cerberus, Jimmy12345, KeepingAwake, Lars and the rest — for contributing to my web of madness over the years.

Bump, Brian and Welch — three souls that would have loved *Lost* had they not determined they'd had enough of entertainment in this dimension.

My wife, Charlotte — for being encouraging and patient while I tried to wedge a book into an already overstuffed life.

My children Kayleigh, Nick, Jon, Ethan and Cassie — for existing and giving a reason to reach a little higher every day.

And, of course, YOU — for thinking we have something interesting to say here.

FOREWORD

By Javier Grillo-Marxuach

Does the world need another book about *Lost*?

Seriously. Even as someone who was intimately involved with the creation of the series, I must confess that I am somewhat stunned by the level of print generated by the show. If you are reading this while standing at the stacks of your local chain store, you're probably trying to figure out whether to buy this book over *The Official Making of Lost, The Unofficial Lost Companion, A Child's Guide To Lost, What Lost Can Tell You About Philosophy, Lost for the Evangelical Christian* and *Why the Buddha Would Have Watched Lost Even Though He Didn't Have Cable.*

Part of the genius of J.J. Abrams and Damon Lindelof's creation is that — in its deliberate pace, the intricacy of its plotting and the wide open spaces it leaves for the fan's mind to run rampant — it can mean many things to many people. Until *Lost* ends and its creators put definite answers to the many questions raised over its run — if they, in fact, ever decide to do that — there is enough noise in the show's signal for anyone of any agenda to make the argument that the show fits their world view . . . which helps to explain why you probably picked this book up from its resting place next to *Lost and Proust: What Swann's Way Can Tell Us About the Hanso Foundation.*

Another part of the genius behind *Lost* is that its creators are born sales-men who know how to spin a yarn, keep the questions alive and create a level of mystery not just for the narrative but for the narrative behind the narrative. Rumor has it that by the time J.J. Abrams took his second meeting with the ABC brass to pitch them the storyline for the *Lost* pilot along with Damon Lindelof, he had already recruited a B-roll camera crew to record the event for the eventual DVD set.

Is it true? Who knows? It *feels* true . . . because, more than anything else, being a fan of *Lost* is an act of faith in the talent of its creators: faith in the idea that a great master plan is unfolding before us, faith in the idea that the producers want to give us an immersive experience both in front of and behind the scenes . . . and, most importantly, faith that we are in the hands of great tale-spinners who know where they are going, and in getting us there, they will do honor to where we have been.

As I write this, *Lost* has two seasons — thirty some-odd episodes to go — before the answers are revealed. I can't imagine that some viewers won't be disappointed (I also imagine that chief among them will be the guy who wrote the evangelical Christian analysis of the show — but that's just a hunch) — and I am dead certain that whatever conclusion the show finds, it will be the topic of much discussion and publication.

None of which answers the question: does the world need another book about *Lost*?

In truth, I can't answer that objectively, because, you see, *Lost* really did eat my life. At least for a while.

From the spring of 2004 — when I was hired to be part of a think-tank of writers tasked with brainstorming ideas to turn J.J. and Damon's pilot script (yes, the one where Jack died at the end of the first act) into a series — through the fall of 2006 (after writing or co-writing seven episodes, serving as supervising producer for two seasons, and co-writing, producing and performing in a massive *Lost*-themed alternate reality game) when I completed my final broadcast in the role of DJ Dan, a conspiracy shock-jock in said alternate reality game, I lived, ate and breathed *Lost*. The experience can probably be best summed up in the words of one of my fellow producers as we stepped up to accept the Emmy Award for Outstanding Drama Series: "the first line of your obituary has just been written."

I gave a lot to *Lost*, and *Lost* returned it in spades of creative satisfaction, awards and accolades, and professional success . . . but among the many things I received from *Lost*, even as it ate my life, one of the best is that it brought me in contact with some of the most active and motivated fans of any show on television.

Lost is a rare phenomenon in that it achieved both runaway mainstream success and cult show status: its mysteries and unique narrative structure are perfectly suited for the kind of rabid attention that only die-hard sci-fi/media fans can provide. *Lost* fans of the cult variety are like cyberpunk Talmudic scholars: poring over every detail, every nuance, meeting in darkened chatrooms over the Internet, writing countless blogs and acting as a kind of "collective detective" — an intellectual force that numbers in the hundreds of thousands, dedicated with an admirable singleness of purpose to deciphering the codes and figuring out the answers to the questions posed by the island.

Lost's fans are at the forefront of a new kind of fandom: they are the beneficiaries of the mainstreaming of sci-fi, the Internet, and the rise of a new wave of *Star Wars*–generation showrunners who are not only web savvy but are also genre fans themselves. These fans have an unprecedented amount of access — not only to behind-the-scenes information, but also to the creators of the shows themselves . . . and that's ultimately what sets this book above the rest. It isn't merely the hagiographic creation narrative of TV's most heavily documented series or a half-baked interpretation of the show's secrets, but the story of how fans, bloggers, netizens, code-freaks, shippers, slashers and photoshop-manippers interact with a television series on the bold frontier of the new-media world . . . written by two authors who have, themselves, made the journey from fans to bloggers to something completely new and different.

So . . . does the world need another book about *Lost*?

Maybe . . . maybe not . . . but the avid fans of *Lost* — those whose faith drive the ongoing buzz on the series — deserve to hear told the story of how their devotion turned not just into ratings, but into the ground zero for a new kind of fandom. It is a story worth reading not just because it relates to *Lost*, but because it describes how television, the Internet and ultimately, the power of storytelling galvanized a group of fans to express themselves on an unprecendeted scale . . . and in its own way, this tale of online message boards, late-night bowling parties, LiveJournal drama and the tension between storytelling, marketing and the fannish desire to play in a shared universe is as interesting as anything that could happen on a strange and mysterious island many, many miles away.

INTRODUCTION

Have you ever been flipping through one of the bazillion books about *Lost* and wished that some genuine *Lost* fans would write a book about the show? Or better yet, about the *Lost* fandom? Well guess what . . . that very thing has happened, and you're holding it in your hands.

Lost Ate My Life is the brainchild of well-known and respected *Lost* blogger Jon "DocArzt" Lachonis, who had approached Nikki Stafford during the off season looking for advice on how to get a *Lost* book project off the ground. As fate would have it, Nikki — who is the author of the finest series of *Lost* books going (*Finding Lost*) — was looking to edit a book for her publisher. The initial pitch was made, everything looked good.

Doc wanted the book to give a truly full picture of the *Lost* fandom, including the interactions between the fans and those people who bring us the show each week. The concept was catchy, Nikki was liking it, but there was a stumbling block. . . . Doc didn't want a book that was strictly from the perspective of a blogger. The last thing he wanted was a monochromatic take on things. To be a true story of the *Lost* fandom, the book needed a wider perspective.

Enter Amy "hijinx" Johnston, who embodies a rare combination in any fandom — a regular fan who just happens to have direct access to people inside *Lost* and Bad Robot Productions. Having gained the trust of *Lost* executive producer Bryan Burk early in the first season of the show, hijinx was known to have regular contact with him and other members of the *Lost* creative team. As well, she is a long-time member and ultra-moderator on The Fuselage (www.thefuselage.com), the official site for *Lost*'s creative team that is sponsored by J.J. Abrams himself. Doc first became aware of hijinx and her connections through her Evil Puppet Masters blog (www.evilpuppetmasters.com), and he friended her on MySpace. They exchanged some e-mails that eventually led to hijinx doing some freelance writing for BuddyTV, which Doc was writing for at that time.

They had been friends for about a year when, in August of 2007, hijinx mentioned to Doc in an IM session that one of her contacts at *Lost*, Gregg Nations, had told her that she should write a book about the *Lost* fandom. Doc's response was, "Funny you should mention writing a book. . . ." He told her about his idea to do just that, but he wasn't sure he had enough material on his own to fill a publishable book. He asked if she would be interested in collaborating, and her answer was a definite "*Yes.*"

The book you are holding is the result of that collaboration. We, the authors, didn't want to cover the same material that other *Lost* books have covered. There are no episode guides or deep discussions regarding the philosophical implications of science vs. faith here. This is the inside story of a fandom, the likes of which has not been seen before, and the show that spawned it. We talk about *Lost* from the perspective of two fans who have had their fingers on the pulse of its fandom since the very beginning. We tell stories that most journalists can't, because we are — first and foremost — fans. We know what "shippers" are. We know who Darlton is. We have been to Destination: L.A. and LOST Weekend. We have even visited the Hawaii set and the offices of *Lost* Labs. We were able to arrange for interviews with executive producers, writers and actors from the show. Even the photos in this book are all taken by fans — they have not been published anywhere else.

But fandom alone isn't enough to drive a book like this, and we know it. So the more subtle aspects of the *Lost* story are inspected alongside the interfacing of the fan community. What is it about this show that draws us all in? Is it a valid phenomenon, or just a pop-culture flash in the pan? . . . Trust us. They mean it. They really mean it.

Lost fans will recognize the common vernacular of people who talk about the show online and by the watercooler. Any industry people who pick this book up will get the closest look at how a fandom thinks, lives and breathes than has ever been put in print before. This book tears down the wall between Hollywood and the fans — just like *Lost* did.

PART 1

Chapter 1

HOW *LOST* ALMOST
WENT *NOWHERE*

SOMEWHERE OVER THE PACIFIC OCEAN, between the United States and Australia, a commercial airliner has developed a series of problems. The navigation equipment is off-line, and the transponders are not functioning. To make matters worse, the pilot cannot achieve radio contact with the ground. Tensions mount while the oblivious passengers continue on with mundane flight rituals, without even the slightest idea that the plane they are in will soon crash. Among the passengers are a doctor, a conman, a pregnant girl, a drug addict, a spoiled rich girl, a fugitive and several others who will soon become the only survivors of the doomed flight.

If you think you know where the story is going, think again. In this story, the passengers don't find themselves on a mysterious island that seems imbued with a mystical presence, there are no monsters that thrash through the jungles, and there is no Dharma Initiative. The story is *Nowhere* and this is the tale of how *Lost* almost went *Nowhere*.

Lloyd Braun did not start his entertainment career as a "creator" of shows. As an entertainment industry lawyer, Braun handled the behind-the-scenes legalese for such luminaries as Larry David and David Chase. Larry David would later cement his affinity with Braun by creating the character of "Lloyd Braun" for *Seinfeld*. Shortly after helping Chase bring *The Sopranos* into existence, Braun drifted into the world of television full-time in 2002 as chairman of ABC.

Around a year into his tenure, ABC was lagging in the network ratings race. Desperate to reverse its fortunes, the network gathered its executives for a brainstorming retreat. While there, each retreat participant was expected to come up with an idea for a show. Braun chose the concept behind the Tom Hanks film *Cast Away*, a move anyone would surely reject as typical Hollywood cookie-cutter decision making. Still, the idea must have held tremendous promise at the time. *Cast Away* was an air disaster that held an almost archetypal charm that is the antithesis to the still-fresh horrors of 9/11. The concept of survival, starting over and redemption seemed a cathartic and promising message of hope for television viewers.

According to television industry mythology, the idea met with resistance and even ridicule when Braun's back was turned, but he was the boss, so, as you already know, the show moved forward. At this point, the project wasn't called *Lost*; it probably didn't have a name outside of something like "Lloyd's *Cast Away* knockoff idea," or "island adventure." What it certainly did not include was anything about smoke monsters, flashbacks or mysterious, disembodied whispers. With the backing of Lloyd Braun and ABC senior vice president Thom Sherman, the stranded-on-an-island story went into the development phase. The first version of the story came from the hallowed halls of Aaron Spelling, via the mind of a young writer named Jeffrey Lieber. Though Lieber gave it the name *Nowhere*, it seemed to be going *somewhere* fast.

The story of *Nowhere*'s careful and detail-oriented development process is the antithesis of that of *Lost*'s rushed creation. Spelling and Lieber were determined to create a shockingly realistic story featuring an ensemble of characters weathering arduous circumstances. As the hope of rescue fades, the survivors begin to jockey for control of the micro-civilization that forms on the island. Spelling went as far as to bring in consultants from *National Geographic* to help Lieber develop the locale. Lieber had immersed himself in some of the more popular desert island books like *Lord of the Flies* and *Robinson Crusoe*.

When Lieber's first draft of *Nowhere* was turned in, ABC's executives were enthusiastic, but thought it needed another pass. Snippets of the script that have appeared online show an eerily toned character piece steeped with hyper-realistic exposition. One of the characters is a military officer with some experience in crash recovery. This is the sort of move you can get away with on TV, kind of like having the villain start spouting his motivation in the final act. What is immediately clear from Lieber's writing of this character is that he wanted the realism so badly that he was willing to resort to exposition to get it.

Between a scene aboard the plane that walks us through the technical problems in excruciating detail and the blatant exposition of our crash recovery expert General White, there is little mystery left as to what happened to the plane or why it will never be found. These questions are the lifeblood of *Lost*, even if the reason for the crash was eventually revealed. In an interview with *Chicago Magazine* (August 2007), Lieber insisted that in *his* story rescue and escape were concepts that needed to be snuffed out as soon as possible. "The biggest challenge with the show was removing, for the most part, the idea that these people would be saved any time soon. One doesn't want to have to spend every episode dwelling on 'rescuers' or plans of escape."

The result is characters enacting conversations that seem to be culled from the front of a first-time viewer's mind. For instance, in this scrap of dialogue between one of two brothers that survived the crash and our aforementioned crash recovery expert, General White seems all too ready to insert some good questions of his own to Truman's inquiry, along with some peculiarly precise statistics:

```
                    TRUMAN
How long do you think it'll take someone to find
us?


                 GENERAL WHITE
Depends. Was the plane off course when we went
down? If so, how far? Were the transponders
```

functioning? I'm sure there are rescue teams
looking for us, but there are a million square
miles of ocean between Australia and South
America. God only knows where they're looking.

                    TRUMAN
So . . . days? Weeks?

                    GENERAL WHITE
When I was doing search and rescue, I'd sit new
recruits down and go over the numbers. Ninety
percent of airplane crash survivors and victims
are found within twenty-four hours . . . eight
percent within seventy-two . . . two percent
within a week.

As utilitarian as this passage may be, it is not necessarily the yardstick
for the script. The story is packed with some genuinely chilling moments. For
instance, in one scene, one of the children — yes, there are children in this version of *Lost* — excitedly tells the adults that she saw more survivors swimming
ashore. When the adults arrive at the beach, they find it littered with the rotting
remains of less fortunate crash victims who didn't fair quite as well. We see an
echo, albeit probably not an intentional one, in the later episode of *Lost*'s second season "The Other 48 Days," in which Mr. Eko gathers the Oceanic Flight
815 dead from the water.

Whether he was deceived by merely casual interest, or was out-and-out
misled, Lieber believed *Nowhere* was on the verge of going into production,
with him as the creator. Braun was apparently happy with the script, although
according to most reports he had never talked directly with Lieber, and the pilot
was sent back for another round of polishing. Lieber was exasperated, but such
is the life of a Hollywood scribe. The day before he was to turn in his final
draft, ABC dropped a bombshell on Lieber and Spelling. *Nowhere* was now going
nowhere.

If you have the opening credits of *Lost* imprinted on your cerebral cortex like most of us *Lost* fans do, you probably have the notion that the story doesn't end there. And you're correct. Jeffrey Lieber, after all, is listed in the credits as one of the creators of the show. That may seem fitting, in some ways. Lieber did a tremendous amount of work on a show about some plane crash survivors, many of whose character outlines sound quite familiar. There are other similarities, too. In Lieber's *Nowhere* the only part of the plane to make land is the fuselage.

But these similarities are superficial at best. "Stranded on an island" stories were once considered a genre all their own. In literature, tales of castaways conquering harsh untamed worlds were the canvas of a significant number of early adventure novels. Inspired by the true stories of early castaways like Gonzalo de Vigo, Juan de Cartagena and Pedro Sánchez Reina, usually criminals or mutineers purposely set adrift who later become enlightened and redeemed through the rigors of their isolation, Daniel Defoe set about writing *Robinson Crusoe*. Although clearly borrowing themes from Shakespeare's *The Tempest*, written a full century earlier, and even earlier works such as the 11th century *Alive, Son of Wake*, and *Theologus Autodidactus* (which, as we'll show later, come close to containing the full set of *Lost*'s more unique elements), Defoe pared away the Bard's signature fanciful and otherworldly mythological tones for a more bare story of a man alone against a strange and forbidding microworld.

The Crusoe story so fascinated readers of the age that the literary genre of "Robinsonade" sprang to existence, with its multitude of Defoe knockoffs, to satiate the thirst for more tales of protagonists adrift, alone, left to find their

>: "Moon - Congrats. You have officially stumbled on to not only my game plan on this board, but the game plan of LOST. Your reward will be for me to tell you what the monster is. So without further ado… The monster is… Wait. Hold on. My phone's ringing. I'll be right back."
- Damon Lindelof, 12/22/04

>: "Betsy - Thanks - and rest assured, THE MONSTER WILL RETURN. PS: Then again, there are no such things as monsters."
- J.J. Abrams, 12/13/04

>: "Oh, man… BIGFOOT is SO on the island."
- Damon Lindelof, 11/25/04

(All quotations from TheFuselage.com)

The Characters Who Almost Went Nowhere

Were these characters the influence for some of our Losties? Decide for yourself.

Truman Graham (Age 28): Rough-around-the-edges "leader" type.

Zach Tyne (19): Young, strapping surfer-type with a penchant for heavy metal.

Sarah Hill (38): Beautiful brunette on the cusp of middle age.

Paul Hill: Sarah's husband; he doesn't make it.

Xander Britzke (32): An Australian playboy on his way to San Francisco.

Piper Brightman (18): Blonde vixen with a slightly spoiled side.

Ed Heinz (32): A mountainous (but not particularly jovial) presence.

General Frank White: An older, bordering on geriatric, man with a philosophical side. His knowledge of search and rescue makes him somewhat of a statesman to the other survivors.

Ross Porter (30): Arguably, the younger version of Thurston Howell III from *Gilligan's Island*. A spoiled rich boy anxious to prove his worth.

wits or perish. The Robinsonade movement was no flash in the pan, either. Robinsonades continue to be produced to this day in the literary world, one of the most recent being Yann Martel's *Life of Pi*, released in September of 2001.

As it turns out, whether intended or not, Braun's inclination to build a television show around the mythology of *Cast Away* was a far safer bet than any of the executives could have figured. Our fascination with the redemption and even enlightenment of a character stranded on a deserted island (or even in the belly of a whale) is an enduring one. With a literary history stretching back hundreds of years, it would seem that when a fan becomes engrossed in a story like *Lost*, or even *Nowhere*, it might be an unconscious reflex.

Perhaps it was the rigid confines of *Nowhere*'s premise that initially turned off J.J. Abrams when Braun approached him about rescuing the fast-sinking project. Abrams would only proceed if the story could have supernatural overtones. Already busy with other projects, Abrams was soon buoyed when Damon Lindelof was introduced as a potential collaborator. Possessing a healthy dose of sci-fi geek cred, Lindelof energized Abrams' approach. The two dove headfirst into the creation of an alternate outline to Braun's pitch. Unlike Lieber's carefully plotted, fact-checked realism that took weeks and weeks of careful research and prepping, Lindelof and Abrams produced their first outline of the pilot after just a week of late-night cramming sessions. In contrast to Braun's tepid response to Lieber's *Nowhere*, his response this time was beyond enthusiastic. The executive, who in the meanwhile had found himself on the tightrope with Disney's senior management, declared the outline the best piece of television ever created. Backed by the largest budget in the history of television pilots, 13 million dollars, *Lost*'s breakneck,

J.J. Abrams signs autographs for fans at Destination: LA 1.

hijinx with Thom Sherman, who helped to get *Lost* on our television screens.

11-week production was off and running. Lieber and Spelling's *Nowhere* seemed destined to fade from TVscape's collective memory.

In reality, Lieber never asked for the lion's share of the creator credit that he received. Concerned that he was not being fairly compensated or credited for his work on the story that, like it or not, had some modicum of influence on what would later become *Lost*, Lieber filed a grievance with the WGA (Writers Guild of America). In Lieber's own words, he never sought to lay claim to the work of Abrams and Lindelof, just to be recognized as having created a part of the DNA of the show. The question of the correctness of Lieber's claim is, at some level, a philosophical argument. This literary movement that has, in various forms, been burned into the collective unconscious of virtually every society on earth, and expressed in hundreds of folk stories, novels, movies, comic books and sitcoms, suddenly seemed to be the claim of three writers, or at least one.

Fans have argued that while some of the characters in *Nowhere* are similar to those of *Lost*, the collection looks more like a generic assortment of dull modern archetypes that anyone could have come up with. Beyond their topical similarity, there is nothing functional shared between the characters in *Nowhere* and those in *Lost*. Still, Lieber was convinced that the blood of his *Nowhere* could be found in the veins of *Lost*, and with ABC seeking a clean break, he created a memo detailing the similarities, and submitted it along with his grievance to the WGA.

The contents of that memo have never been published.

In the end, it is probably diplomatic caution that caused the Guild to find in Lieber's favor. Lieber had worked on a script that featured an ensemble cast stranded on an island with no hope of rescue; the very premise that had seemed too generic for Abrams and Lindelof was nonetheless a major part of their script.

Nonetheless, the WGA ruled that not only did Lieber deserve credit, but the majority of it. An independent council, whose identity has been kept secret, awarded Lieber 60 percent of the creator credit, determining that the scribe not only receive billing but the largest "creator" share. Lieber would later recall sitting nervously next to Lindelof at the 2005 Emmy Awards. Along with Lindelof and Abrams, Lieber had been nominated for the pilot — more specifically for providing the "story" of *Lost*. Since that time it has hardly mattered what happened before Lindelof and Abrams sat down to meld minds in the common purpose of honing *Lost*'s real story. Like the hundreds of Robinsonades that came before it, it is that wide divide between more typical castaway stories, better represented by *Nowhere*, and *Lost*'s unique landscape that will decide its place in TV history. What cannot be denied is the indelible impression that *Lost* itself has made on the fandom — an impression that has been deepened by the World Wide Web.

Chapter 2

ALL *LOST* FORUMS
ARE NOT CREATED EQUAL

THE INTERNET HAS MADE THE WORLD a much smaller place. There was once a great wall between Hollywood studios and the audiences they tried to reach. Being a fan of a television show meant watching it and hoping that the Nielsen families agreed with your favorites, so it would not be canceled. If you wanted an autographed picture of your favorite actor, you scoured the magazines for fan club information or studio addresses. Things are different now.

The wall that exists between Hollywood and the television audience has become more permeable, especially for the *Lost* fandom. *Lost* fans are a diverse group and arguably some of the most intelligent fans you will ever encounter. The show has spawned many websites that provide venues to discuss every aspect of it — from episode developments to hidden "Easter eggs" to theories to spoilers to casting rumors to so much more. Of all of these online forums connecting *Lost* fans from around the globe, one stands above the rest: The Fuselage (http://www.thefuselage.com). What is it about The Fuselage that distinguishes it from all the other bulletin boards that are equally devoted to *Lost*? Within the realm of The Fuselage, the wall that typically separates the show's creators and its fans is practically nonexistent. The Fuselage has allowed for an open door of communication, where fans can ask questions directly to people who actually work on or act in the show — and those same people answer their questions.

The Fuselage is sponsored by J.J. Abrams and can bill itself as "The Official Site of the Creative Team Behind ABC's Award Winning TV Show 'Lost.'" Why would Abrams support this independently run site that is otherwise unaffiliated with ABC or the production companies that bring us *Lost*? It all started with Fury. David Fury, that is. During the first season of *Lost*, Fury was on staff as a writer and co-executive producer of the show. Fury had been a frequent visitor to another posting board, known as The Bronze: Beta (http://www.bronzebeta.com), that Karri Phillips and Artie McDonald had designed for fans of the television shows *Buffy the Vampire Slayer* and *Angel*. A number of the writers from those two shows, and sometimes even Joss Whedon himself, would post there with the fans. When Fury joined *Lost*, he e-mailed Karri and Artie asking if they would do a site for this new show much like The Bronze: Beta site. He then talked to Abrams about the site, and Abrams agreed to sponsor it — which gave it that rare but oh-so-important "official" title and drew in more people affiliated with *Lost* (known as very important posters, or "VIPS," on the board).

The Fuselage went live in October 2004, a month after *Lost* premiered. The Bronze: Beta had been strictly a linear board, and The Fuselage was the same in the beginning. A "linear board" (or "LB" as it is nicknamed) is an old-fashioned scrolling board that resembles a continuous conversation. People jump in and out, all day long, all night long, from all over the world, and post messages to each other. Whenever a VIP jumps on, there is typically a flood of posts as the "lurkers" decide to chime in and try to get some attention from the VIP. The VIPS generally enjoy the fact that they can sign in at almost any time of the day or night and find *Lost* fans to interact with. But some of the VIPS also wanted a venue wherein fans could leave them questions that they could answer at their leisure, without having to keep up with the constant flow of the LB; thus the addition of a threaded board to The Fuselage. The "threaded board," or "TB" as it is referred to on the site, is set up like any other bulletin board on the Web. The difference being that on The Fuselage, the TB has a section that includes forums for individual VIPS — if a fan wants to ask a question or leave a message for a VIP from the show, they go to his or her forum and start a new thread. Only the VIP and that fan can post replies in that question thread, which prevents other fans from "thread-jacking."

Anyone affiliated with *Lost*, whether they be a writer, producer, actor or otherwise on the *Lost* payroll, who wants to participate on The Fuselage needs only to make a request to Karri Phillips or, during the first season of the show, tell David Fury. After Fury left, executive producer Bryan Burk took over the verification process of the VIPs. All VIPs have to be verified before they are given "color" and a forum. Once verified, a font color is chosen, so as to identify that person's status as a VIP on the board. The only other members of The Fuselage who are allowed to post with a colored font are the administrators and the ultra-moderators. VIPs also choose a posting name — some post under their real name; some choose an alias, like a regular member of the board. Co-creator Abrams and script coordinator Gregg Nations post under their full names: "JJ Abrams" and "Gregg Nations." But Burk and showrunner/writer/co-creator Damon Lindelof post under their nicknames, "Burky" and "The Nomad," respectively. The actors tend to be a bit more creative, with Jorge Garcia posting as "ThinkImGonnaHurley" and Dominic Monaghan as "David St. Hubbins" (the name of the lead singer for the mock rock band Spinal Tap). Another choice that the VIPs make when joining The Fuselage is whether they prefer to post on the LB, the TB or both. Every VIP is given his or her own forum on the TB, but not every VIP uses these personal forums; some choose to jump into the perpetual conversation on the LB whenever they have a chance to come online. The busier VIPs, like Abrams, Lindelof and Burk, tend to prefer the LB, while Nations is strictly a TB poster. Garcia and Terry O'Quinn (John Locke, who posts as "oquinn") are most active in their TB forums, but also occasionally pop up on the LB to have a real-time conversation with the fans.

Javier Grillo-Marxuach was sitting in his office early in season 1 of *Lost* when David Fury poked his head in and told him about The Fuselage, mentioned that J.J. was sponsoring it, gave a little background on its predecessor, The Bronze: Beta, and encouraged him to join the board. For "Javi," as he is called, it was a no-brainer: he had always been Internet savvy and involved in the fandoms of the various shows he had written for over the years. He became a regular poster on the LB, usually popping in during his lunch break from the "Writers' Room." For the first year and a half of The Fuselage's existence, Javi was undeniably the most active VIP, and he embraced The Fuselage wholeheartedly. He kept up with the lingo that online fans of every show use amongst themselves; he has a laminated GEEK card and is blessed with a quick wit that found a perfect fit on the LB, where conversation is usually fast and snarky. After season 2, Javi moved on to other projects, including writing for the television show *Medium*. He also saw his own show green-lighted by ABC Family, *The Middleman*, which is based on his popular comic book series of the same name. He still keeps in touch with some of the regular "Lagers" from The Fuselage and each year shows up at the annual Bowlapalooza competition between his fan club, known as the "javiminions," and *Lost* executive producer Bryan Burk's fan club, the "Burky Babes." His influence on the development of the show's characters and the foundation of the show's fandom is still felt today.

During the first season of *Lost*, the number of VIPs who came to The

Matt Ragghianti, writer's assistant during the first two seasons of *Lost*, logs onto The Fuselage during Destination: LA 1.

Fuselage was astounding. Sometimes they even used the site to communicate with each other. But season 1 was a simpler time in the *Lost* universe — both for the VIPs and for the fans. It was before the mass marketing, before the mass merchandising, before the massive expectations had truly taken hold. Everything was new, fresh and exciting, and the show had discovered mass appeal along with a cult-like following, which took the television industry and the show's own producers by surprise. The Fuselage was swarming with writers and producers, who were all eager to meet and chat with the inaugural fans of the show, so it was here that the roots of the *Lost* fanbase were formed and cultivated — both sides benefiting from this freedom and personal interaction. Fans who were a part of The Fuselage at that time, and who are still a part of the show's fandom today, are some of the most fiercely loyal fans around.

The Fuselage provides a safe haven for the VIPs, a fact that is not always

Former *Lost* scribe Javier Grillo-Marxuach and current *Lost* script coordinator and writer Gregg Nations have both been very active at The Fuselage over the years.

understood or appreciated by the fans who post there. The site's rules are strict, much more rigid and harsh than any other *Lost* fan forum. But the rules serve their purpose: they make the VIPs feel comfortable, allow them to interact at will with the fans, maintain their privacy and protect them from tactless wackos. And yes, all fandoms have wackos. The moderators of The Fuselage have a truly thankless job, and it is a job for which they are not compensated. The work can easily consume their lives, and so, from time to time, a moderator has to take a "hiatus." The notion of "attack the post, not the poster" is pretty much a rule on every forum on the Internet, but it is sometimes hard to not take certain comments personally. For a board with over 60,000 registered members, approximately 10,000–20,000 of which are active members (depending on whether or not the show is in season), the policing of the board rests on the shoulders of a couple of administrators, four ultra-moderators, two super-moderators and a dozen or so mini-moderators. No one can empathize with

Fuselager Susan (velton) painted this visual interpretation of the S.S.C.C. (Sawyer's Southern Comfort Club), the virtual hangout for those Fusers who like to participate on the linear board.

a Fuselage moderator save another Fuselage moderator.

As the years and seasons of *Lost* have passed, The Fuselage has changed along with the show. The size of the show's marketing presence and the size of the fandom have grown exponentially, causing a dilution of The Fuselage's concentration and intimacy. The Fuselage was and still is the very heart of the fandom; practically every other popular *Lost* site, whether it be a forum, blog or informational site, sprouted from its beating core. Fans initially come to "the Fuse" or "the Lage" in awe, amazed that they can actually post directly to a VIP — a real live conduit to this amazing show. Over time, that awe has faded into complacency, with some posters feeling somewhat superior to those *Lost* fans who are either new to the Fuse or who do not frequent it at all. Though unattractive, it is debatable that this arrogance has been earned. If you have been with The Fuselage for an extended length of time and have been an active par-

>: "Cheri: I love that The Fuselage has taken off. It was important to me that we have a place where fans can hang. Much credit goes to Fury, who turned me on to the idea."
— J.J. Abrams, 4/8/06

>: And BIGGEST love to all of you guys. Can't tell you how much it means to drop by the 'lage and get the honest and loving feedback from the most devoted devotees of our little island adventure. Until we meet again, Peace out!"
— Damon Lindelof, 10/12/06

>: "I love The Fuselage. It's the only place Damon and I actually get to TALK."
— J.J. Abrams, 11/4/04

>: "And J.J.'s not kidding about how we don't talk except for when we post together. I'm sitting in his lap right now."
— Damon Lindelof, 11/4/04

(All quotations from TheFuselage.com)

ticipant on the LB or in the VIP forums on the TB, chances are you have had direct contact with people directly involved in making *Lost*. It is tough not to feel that you deserve some bragging rights if you asked Nations or Garcia or O'Quinn a question and they responded to you, or if you managed to get a shout-out from Lindelof on the LB.

Gregg Nations joined the *Lost* creative team after season 1 as a script coordinator, which is when he first heard about The Fuselage from a couple of the writers' assistants. Initially skeptical of its claim of being an "official" site, Gregg poked around the forums a bit to see what the site was all about. When he finally got confirmation from both Lindelof and Javi that the site was legit and that they both posted there, Gregg signed up.

As the seasons of *Lost* have progressed and a number of the posting VIPS have become too busy to visit The Fuselage anymore or have moved on to other projects, Nations' presence has become more obvious and his Q&A forum is the most active of the creative team VIP forums. He learned quickly that he has to consider every word that he posts very carefully. Nations remembers once going into his forum and noticing that the number of views for one particular answered thread was over 1,000 — and was being discussed in other threads on the board. He had a panicked moment, wondering what he had said to elicit such interest from the fans. As he put it, "That taught me to be cautious about the way I answered questions, to be as clear as I could . . . or to be purposefully vague."

Now Nations' evasive and snarky responses are a thing of legend at The Fuselage. There is even a thread dedicated to his own "Greatest Hits" — some zinger responses that are too good not to be repeated and shared. Late in season 3, his most oft-used phrase was "Wait, watch and see." With the preponderance of answers that were dished out on the show in season 4, that was definitely sage advice.

It is well known by those who frequent the LB that Damon Lindelof likes to lurk on new episode nights while the show is airing live in the Eastern and Central time zones. He used to have the time to pay The Fuselage a rather lengthy visit, answering questions and participating in the witty banter that runs rampant there. Nowadays he usually posts only once or twice after the episode has aired, but that is more than enough to make the LB Fusers feel a sense of power, knowing that the showrunner himself may be reading their reactions to an episode in real time. In one of the official *Lost* podcasts, Lindelof explained his preference for The Fuselage over other sites: "There is a board called thefuselage.com which I frequent and [it is] actually made up of fans of the show that [are] more fun and enthusiastic, and less on the negative axis." He calls these fans "the loyalest of the loyal," and he has come to recognize the names of the regulars, going so far as to engage with those who always come on to criticize, as well. Sometimes he will offer a tidbit about a future episode, but usually he is thanking these fans for their loyalty and praising the various writers, directors and actors whose talents were showcased in that particular episode. Despite his busy schedule, Lindelof is still more present for his show's fans than practically every other television showrunner out in Hollywood manages to be.

During the first season of *Lost*, a particularly devout group of fans of the show bonded on the LB of The Fuselage. Through all the twists and turns of the show, through Dharma stations and reruns, this was the group of fans who "got it." Damon calls this group "the faithful" but they call each other the "Usual Suspects," and all have friendships that have gone beyond the black-and-green backdrop of The Fuselage. They try to welcome the new posters, hold their hands and point them to the FAQs, but after almost four years and a long history of inside jokes amongst them, it is admittedly unusual to find oneself accepted into their fold. The Usual Suspects are aware of their elite-ness: there is no list of members anywhere, but they know who they are. They have been posting on the Fuse long enough to remember when the LB was filled with a rainbow of colored fonts. They have questioned and goofed off with not only Javi and Damon, but J.J., Burky and various writers from seasons past. A few cast members have jumped on the LB over the years, as well — Terry O'Quinn and Jorge Garcia being the most active, with a few memorable appearances by Dominic Monaghan, Ian Somerhalder (Boone), Maggie Grace (Shannon) and Daniel Dae Kim (Jin), as well. The Usual Suspects trust "*Lost* Labs" (a fandom term that refers to members of *Lost*'s creative team, mainly the writers of the show), and Lindelof trusts them in return. He knows that their criticisms, while vocal, will be constructive rather than destructive or personal.

While Lindelof lurks on the LB during the episode, Nations is typically patrolling the "Watching Live" thread on the TB where viewers can log on to describe and comment on the show as they watch it. The choice of these VIPs to come to The Fuselage to gauge the fandom's reaction to a new episode solidifies this site's high rank among the *Lost* websites. Not even the "official" bulletin board for the show on ABC's site has that kind of clout.

At the first *Lost* fan party held in April 2005, known as "Destination: L.A. 1" (or DLA1), Lindelof spoke to the crowd, which was mainly made up of Fuselagers and people affiliated with the show or with Abrams' production company Bad Robot, gathered in a ballroom at the Hollywood and Highland Center at the Renaissance Hotel in Los Angeles. He mentioned that just a few short years before *Lost*, he was exactly like the fans in the crowd: he went to discussion boards to talk with fellow fans about his favorite television shows. The Internet savvy of Damon Lindelof and some of the other VIPs definitely contributed to their understanding of how powerful and important a website like The Fuselage could be as a direct link between the show's creators and fans — and now is. Some fans misconstrue their direct interaction with VIPs as evidence that they have more power than they actually do within the walls of the *Lost* Writers' Room. But outside of this minority, most of the fans who have become members of The Fuselage come away from their experiences there with a broader and deeper understanding of the show and those who bring it to us.

Chapter 3

TO SPOIL OR
NOT TO SPOIL?

ANY TV SHOW THAT has a reasonably active online presence will attract spoilers. *Lost* is no exception. But due to the abundance of questions raised by the plot — some of which are not answered for *seasons* — and the imminent threat of demise for any character on the show, even the major characters, spoilers for *Lost* can actually ruin the enjoyment of the show for some viewers. What leads a fan to seek out a spoiler, even if they are told it could ruin the episode or story arc for them? Why do people within the industry share copyrighted information that they have signed confidentiality agreements to protect? Is a fan who seeks spoilers a true fan of the show? Is a fan who spreads spoilers the antichrist?

First and foremost, Damon Lindelof absolutely *hates* spoilers. And not just the usual leaks from anonymous sources within the crew or in post-production — he has expressed his dislike for even the teasers that ABC shows for the next episode. That is evidence of just how diverse the definition of a spoiler can be — even within the marketing of the show itself. ABC wants to tease the audience so that they will tune in the next week. Sometimes what they choose to show in the teaser exposes the culmination of a story arc that Damon Lindelof and *Lost*

Labs have been building towards for half a season. Damon's ire was most heard in the first two seasons, when it seemed that every week the teasers were giving us reveals that a lot of fans would rather not know about before the episode actually aired. Lindelof was not always aware of what the teaser showed, so, often, he would log on to The Fuselage and ask the east coast viewers what was in the teaser.

Some fans do not want to know anything about an unaired episode before they see it live. These "spoilerphobes" go to extremes — turning off the television as soon as an episode ends, so they won't even see the teaser for the next episode; avoiding television gossip shows and magazine articles that typically cover *Lost*; and even avoiding the Internet completely — especially during the weeks leading up to a season finale — all for fear of being spoiled accidentally. This may seem like they are overdoing it, but to these spoilerphobes the most important thing is being able to watch each episode in its purest form — as the creators designed it to be seen. They appreciate the crafting of the story as it is contained within the act breaks (i.e., breaks for commercials). They can focus on what is happening *now* on the show, rather than looking for clues to what they have heard will happen two episodes down the road.

The group of *Lost* fans who classify themselves as "spoilerholics" have a wide variety of reasons for seeking out spoilers. They look for the puzzle pieces embedded in the show that foreshadow big events. To them, watching the show is just one part of a larger game. Other spoilerholics just do not like to be surprised — they find comfort in knowing the resolution of the cliffhangers days, weeks or even months before the episode airs. While the spoilerphobes had no idea that Shannon was going to be shot until it happened, the spoiler addicts knew and were already theorizing the repercussions for Ana Lucia well before the episode even aired.

One of the trickier aspects of spoilers is how they are obtained. Since so much of *Lost* is filmed outdoors, a number of residents of and vacationers to Hawaii have managed to capture photos of scenes being shot. The on-set crew and extras have been known to pass along information, which is true for most television shows, even though these people are all required to sign nondisclosure agreements and they can be fired if they are discovered to be the source of the leak.

Throughout seasons 1 and 2 of *Lost*, the mainstream media pretty much had their way with *Lost*. The show's nature as a mystery-infused, relentless cliff-hanger brought even casual fans to the Internet after each episode hungry for clues that they may have missed, theories that seemed to make sense, and, of course, the bits of information leaked to the press about upcoming episodes. Two of the most active providers of this material were Kristin Veitch of E! (now known as Kristin Dos Santos) and *TV Guide*'s Michael Ausiello.

Using sources at various levels of production, the two jockeyed for position as spoiler hunters extraordinaire. In any given week, their columns would reveal major plot points of upcoming episodes, effectively defusing some of the show's biggest short-term mysteries. The more accurate the spoilers became, the more the fans wanted them.

Michael Ausiello's philosophy on why fans are so rabidly interested in spoilers goes like this: "People are impatient. They don't want to wait to find out what's going to happen on their favorite shows. If they're invested in a particular story or couple, they want a warning that the rug is about to get pulled out from under them. Also, there's something exciting about finding out stuff before you're supposed to. It's sort of like when you're a kid and you ransack the house looking for your Christmas gifts. You know what you're doing is wrong but you just can't help yourself!" The thrill is in the pursuit of something that you're not supposed to have.

Ausiello also knows firsthand how powerful the desire for information can be. When their demands for information are not met, spoilerholics are quick to chastise the writer. "What I find is you're 'damned if you do and damned if you don't.' If you disguise a spoiler hangman-style behind a series of asterisks — for example, 'Aaron is *** *** of the Oceanic Six' — they're pissed at you for not just revealing it outright. But then if you reveal it outright, they're pissed at you for spoiling it. I'm constantly in search of the middle ground that will please everyone." It is a futile pursuit. As executive producers Carlton Cuse and Damon Lindelof have said on numerous occasions, it is impossible to please every *Lost* fan.

On September 7, 2006, a few weeks prior to the season 3 premiere of *Lost*, Gregg Nations responded to a question about spoilers in his Q&A thread on The

Fuselage with a hypothetical story that turned out to be not so hypothetical after all. The gist of it was that some intentionally false casting breakdown sheets had been sent out by *Lost* Labs in an effort to track the resulting spoilers that would inevitably come out — thus revealing the source of the leak. The resulting "foilers" (fake spoilers) left some members of the fan community feeling hurt and angry. They felt as if *Lost* Labs was trying to punish the spoilerholics. In fact, the intent was to find the person or persons on the *Lost* payroll who was breaking their confidentiality agreement. It was a business decision, not an anti-spoiler vendetta. Nations caught a good deal of flak from the angry fans who felt they had been "lied to" by the creative team. But that's just it, the lies were directed at those actually starting the spoilers, not those who read them. The spoilerholics were just swept up in the wake of the foilers.

By the time season 3 premiered, Lindelof and Co. had sewn up most of the leaks attributed to on-set sources. They were able to keep a lock on the major surprise in the season 3 finale episode, "Through the Looking Glass," right up until approximately two weeks before the episode aired. That would have been at the point when the episode left the tight-knit group at *Lost* Labs and was let loose to the network, where it is nearly impossible to keep track of how many pairs of hands the episode passes through. Right about that time, a full synopsis was leaked, and along with it the details of the "snake in the mailbox," the codeword for season 3's gamechanger, the revelation that Jack's "flash" was taking place in the future. It was a moment that was designed to knock the wind out of fans and critics alike. This time, though, the spoiler did not come from the mainstream press, but from the fan community. "Darlton" (Damon Lindelof and Carlton Cuse) may have successfully corralled the entertainment media, but there is no controlling the independent *Lost* bloggers and webmasters.

The person who released the synopsis of the episode was only known by his or her online alias: "lostfan108." What might not be well known is that lostfan108 actually offered the information to a handful of well-known *Lost* bloggers, but DarkUFO was the only one to accept the offer. The lostfan108 saga began at the well-known entertainment blog AintItCoolNews (AICN). Initially, the spoilers appeared as a list of not very revealing bulleted points about the episode. Alone, they were fairly innocuous; when mixed with the many contrivances, guesses and less revealing spoilers, however, they formed a much more telling portrayal of the episode. Still, they did not reveal "the snake in the mailbox." As excited commentators tried to intuit the meaning of the cryptic list of points, lostfan108 struck. The first synopsis from lostfan108 appeared in the comment system of AintItCoolNews. It more or less outlined every major revelation in the episode, but trod lightly when it came to "the snake in the mailbox." There, lostfan108 seemed to hesitate. Maybe it was a matter of conscience. In any case, he/she began to asterisk out character names and became increasingly vague. Within hours, the post was gone from AintItCoolNews.com, a site known to be in the good graces of J.J. Abrams. While the full story has never been told, it is assumed that someone from within ABC contacted the writers of AICN and appealed either at a personal or a legal level to have the information removed. But it was too late.

Not happy that his/her spoiler had been removed from AICN, lostfan108 began shopping it around to some of the best known *Lost* blogs on the Web. The Tail Section (www.thetailsection.com) had a shot, and promptly refused. At this point, the synopsis had shed its asterisks and "fill in the blanks" safety catches; instead, it offered all of the information needed to completely spoil one of *Lost*'s most closely guarded secrets.

In the land of *Lost*-related online blogs, DarkUFO is known as a kind of nexus of all that goes on in relation to *Lost*. If news hits the Web, air, radio or TV, it is quickly scraped up and catalogued in one of DarkUFO's numerous categories. There is a certain indiscriminate quality to this round-up; rarely are news items commented on to any great degree but rather pasted in their entirety. DarkUFO, or Andy as his friends know him, leaves most of the commentary to his extremely active and vocal readership.

As the aggregate of all things *Lost*, DarkUFO naturally has cemented itself as one of the best sources for spoilers. Rarely are these spoilers generated from within, but if there is one place where you can find out what E!, TV *Guide* and virtually any other well-connected outlet has spilled from day to day, it is on DarkUFO's spoiler blog. It is the epitome of one-stop shopping.

The backlash against DarkUFO for releasing the season 3 finale synopsis was immediate, on both sides of the argument. A post at the TheTailsection.com condemning the release, entitled "One Rotten Apple," fast became the site's most commented-on article. In it, the writer made this statement: "In their most respectable form, spoilers are tempered to provide provocative ideas about what might happen in an upcoming episode. Occasionally, they give up a specific detail without context, giving us the fuel we need to theorize towards any number of possibilities. In their most despicable form, spoilers deprive us the thrill we would experience when the carefully executed plot reaches its sweet spot. Also, these extreme spoilers cause people to pre-judge a concept of plot without seeing it executed. A sad sad way to evaluate the artistic process of film, or any other medium as far as that goes."

On the pro-spoiler side of the argument, fans talked about spoilers as if the act of withholding them was immoral — at the very least, they feel that any blogger who had information about episodes and did not share it was depriving the community of a deeper appreciation. To these spoilerholics, foreknowledge of an event on the show simply increases the enjoyment of the final execution.

When the fourth season began, the shift of spoiler sourcing from the mainstream to the fan scene was complete. The identity of Jeff Fahey's character's name (Frank Lapidus) was revealed by an intern who pulled it up in Disney's complex project database; images of the exterior of the mysterious "Orchid" hatch made their way onto the Internet well in advance of the season premiere; then with just weeks before the premiere of season 4, the apple cart was toppled yet again. This time, it wasn't the upcoming premiere that would be spoiled, but the fourth episode, "Eggtown." Again, it was a full synopsis, and again it was released by a mysteriously monikered "source" at DarkUFO. For *Lost* script coordinator Gregg Nations, who co-wrote the episode — his first script for *Lost* — this spoiler leak affected him personally. He said, "If it had been one or two plot points, that may not have bothered me, but it was the whole thing, including the surprise ending [discovering Kate's child is actually Aaron]. . . . When it comes to something like that, where you can't trust the people who have [been] brought into the family and contribute to the production in some way, then it's something that cannot be accepted as part of the business." When the regular media, like Dos Santos and Ausiello, had been the ones providing spoilers to the fans, they felt some sense of obligation to avoid a full synopsis of an episode and withhold the major cliffhangers. Why? Because revealing certain information could put them on the bad side of the producers of the show, thus making on-set visits and exclusive interviews difficult to obtain down the road. When spoilers began erupting from the fandom itself, however, that sliver of control that the producers had over the press evaporated.

By this time, the limited availability of season 4 screeners had become a point of contention between the studio and the press. Suddenly fansites were releasing spoilers culled from leaked in-house screeners for the first four episodes, but the press had been left out in the cold. The spoiler hounds were not only upsetting the artistic integrity of the show, they were having an impact on studio/press politics as well.

In the present tense, an unspoiled episode of *Lost* is the equivalent of an unobtainable best-case scenario, and the policing of spoilers is in the hands of the fanbase, since the mainstream has learned, grudgingly, to reign itself

>: "Dearest Friends, A few words on SPOILERS... They suck. 'Nuff said."
— Damon Lindelof, 11/10/05

>: "And dammit... don't trust those crazy promos! I'm not spoiling anything by saying we are VERY cognitive of our bullet counts...
TRUST US.
(at least this once)."
— Damon Lindelof, 11/17/05

>: "Halfrek — You're my hero. Death to Spoilers.

P.S. Charlie dies.

P.S.S. Just kidding.

P.S.S.S. No, I'm not.

P.S.S.S.S. Yeah, I'm kidding."
— Damon Lindelof, 5/16/05

(All quotations from TheFuselage.com)

in. The question now is: should it have ever gotten to the point where spoilers are being entrusted to the fanbase? In the case of *Lost*, the producers' leashing of the mainstream media backfired. With sources like E! and *TV Guide* muzzled, the fan community became desperate for "real" spoilers. In the online world, all it takes is one legitimate spoiler to send a website's hit count through the roof — and for the website owners, hits equal money. For a site such as DarkUFO, which benefits more from its hit count than being in the good graces of ABC, obtaining spoilers — regardless of how explosive — solidifies the site's relevance as the de facto source for spoilers. While Andy (the owner of the DarkUFO blog) has admitted that he himself loathes the ultra-revealing "ruiners," he operates on

Burky and The Nomad answer questions at the first (and only) official *Lost* convention held in June 2005. One thing that is not in question is how Damon feels about spoilers.

Gregg Nations and Bryan Burk address the crowd at LOST Weekend 2007, thanking the fans for their continued love and support.

the notion that if he doesn't publish them someone else will. With no other legitimate press sources to get the "good stuff" from, the spoiler-holics have flocked to his site, much to the chagrin of the show's producers. Now that the floodgate has been opened, there is no way to stem the flow.

The season 4 finale saw the return of the notorious lost-fan108, and a new level of security chez *Lost* that, ultimately, would prove embarrassing for one of the authors of this book (oh okay, it was Doc). Though he'd moved from TheTailsection.com to DocArzt.com, Doc's philosophy of how to publish spoilers had not changed.

Given the opportunity to see much of the season in advance of airtime, along with some on-set access, his code of ethics was different from the mainstream press. At no time does DocArzt.com ask the *Lost* boys if they approve of information being released — but Doc made the decision to exercise restraint with spoilers and help maintain suspense. This is an attitude that comes from respect for the storytelling process as much as it does for the show itself.

When lostfan108 popped up again to spoil the season 4 finale of *Lost*, again choosing DarkUFO as his or her outlet, the creative team had already formed a plan to foil the notorious heckler; a plan they failed to share with some of their most trusted soldiers on the anti-ruiner battlefield.

This time around, the most explosive piece of info was the identity of the person in the coffin. Lostfan108 had given the startling reveal a numbing shot of Novocaine weeks prior to the airing of the episode by revealing that it was John Locke in the coffin. In the meantime, actual footage of the final scene made its way into a certain blogger's hands. That blogger (Doc) saw a very different face in the coffin: Desmond. Lostfan108 had revealed himself to be no longer in the loop. DocArzt.com made the bold claim that lostfan108 had been foiled, in verbiage far too inelegant for this book (but perfectly fine for the salty world of blogs). When it was revealed that it was indeed Locke in the coffin, Doc was subjected to twelve hours of angry spoilerholic ranting on his site. It wasn't until the next morning that the facts behind the foul-up were revealed. The *Lost* producers had gone the extra mile to ensure their secret would remain a secret until the finale aired. Three separate endings had been shot: one with Locke in the casket; one with Sawyer; and one with Desmond.

If there was ever a time when the Svengali-like influence of spoiler superstars like DarkUFO and lostfan108 was demonstrated, it was in the wake of this failed attempt to control those who would prefer we watch the show with half our brain planted in the future. The initial outrage was full of demands for apology from Doc, condemnation and even a few suggestions that this very tome be used as fuel for bonfires. In reality, the challenge to lostfan108's credibility was completely legit given the existence of the alternate endings, but his/her position in the *Lost* food chain was also galvanized since lostfan108 was the only "insider" not to be fooled by the existence of the false endings.

True, lostfan108 had a one-in-three chance of getting it right, but the fact that he or she got it right seemed to narrow the corridor of access that the nefarious ruiner had walked. Lostfan108, after all, had managed to avoid the fake endings (even if the detail that Locke had to be brought back to the island for resurrection was not confirmed in the episode). The lack of subtlety aside, lostfan108 is clearly someone "in the know," but he or she represents the worst impulses that spoiling creates in the fans: the need to jump ahead to the end of the book.

In the end, the question of whether spoilers are good or evil is a pointless discussion. All arguments of logic aside, the phenomenon comes down to a single factor: choice. The reader makes a choice, the reader lives with the consequences of that choice. In the *Lost* community, there will *always* be varying viewpoints on those who come bearing spoilers. They will be the heroes and the villains, the passionate and the dispassionate, the fan and the anti-fan. And then, there will always be those who have no opinion at all. They may check the boards once in a while, find out something before its time, but move on, still breathing, still alive, and find the space to reconnect with the magic that can only occur during the execution of the show.

The actual damage inflicted on the integrity of the *Lost* story may be overstated a lot of times, a by-product of the spoiler's and the spoilee's hyperbole. Each seeks to establish a sense of infamy or outrage out of what, in the end, is just information. To extend the metaphor of *Lost* as a novel, even the most ardent spoilers are only, at best, flipping a few pages ahead.

Chapter 4

WHAT'S IN
THE BOX?

WE SEARCH FOR THE SOURCE of *Lost*'s success like we search for the meaning of life. There is something strangely purposeful — surreal yet oddly familiar — pulsing under the surface of the show, which somehow keeps us tethered to what could just as easily be a forbidding narrative. The base "formula" of *Lost* has not only existed before, but has been duplicated since, yet never to the same level of mastery. What are the "components" to the *Lost* engine that keep us coming back time and time again? Action? Adventure? Suspense? *Lost*'s hold on audiences has been identified as being stronger than can be explained by the draw of mere "pop culture." For the hundreds of thousands of fans who have populated the fan communities, *Lost* has become an institution.

Legitimizing one's interest in the show can be a bit of a challenge. Like all pop culture icons, *Lost* has its detractors. To the average *Lost* hater, we die-hard fans are watching an empty puppet show, mesmerized by the show's constant tease-and-deny tactics, and our only claim to artistic integrity is to insist that there is, in fact, a "man behind the curtain." All *Lost* fans are familiar with the charge that the show is "made up" as it goes along. It is the sort of accusation that suggests *Lost* fans are perhaps a little gullible. That claim may not be so far from the truth in one fundamental regard. At the same time, there is always more to *Lost* than meets the eye at any given moment in the plot, and this reveals a purposely laid groundwork that only reinforces the sense of purpose *Lost* fans believe exists behind the writing of the show.

At a speaking engagement for TED Talks in March of 2007, J.J. Abrams revealed a rather generic-looking box of magic tricks to the audience. Plain white cardboard with an ornate question mark, "Tannen's Magic Mystery Box" spelled out within its curves. The box, Abrams would explain, had never been opened. After pondering why he had never opened the box, Abrams explained that it was because the infinite possibilities of what could be inside the box represented the very essence of imagination. Abrams arrived at the conclusion that sometimes mystery is more important than knowledge. Abrams' speech brought more clarity to the reasons behind the enormous gravity of *Lost* by explaining this one concept, than any number of reveals, theories, symbols or translations to come from the fanbase. *Lost* has achieved the success it has because the creators are experts at presenting the "mystery" in all of its morphic glory. As long as there is the promise of further possibilities, as Abrams suggests, fans will always want to know what is inside the box.

The popular critique that the story is made up on the fly is not entirely a fair assumption. Very early in the series, Lindelof made a post on The Fuselage in response to a question about how the stories come about for each episode. As he put it, ". . . the story process changes from episode to episode. Some are part of the 'master plan' while others are literally broken on the fly. That's the only way to do it in TV." On several occasions either Abrams or Lindelof have openly admitted that the hatch plotline was initially without a resolution. They just liked the idea and weren't sure where to go with it. Lindelof had decided that the hatch would not be introduced in the series until they had worked out that slight detail, but the genesis of it was true to Abrams' magical box philosophy. The fact that the hatch could not be opened became both a catalyst for the sort of infinite possibilities that Abrams talked about as well as a reason *du jour* to support the notion that the writers were winging it. They couldn't open the hatch because the writers didn't know what was in it.

The magic box, as a metaphor, even made its way into the *Lost* canon. In season 3, when Ben Linus suggested that the island was like a "magic box" capable of manifesting whatever anyone desired, synapses began blazing in the fan community. The staple of magic had been a part of the *Lost* DNA from the very beginning. The admission that magic may be "really" going on was fascinating to the fans, many of whom had already made connections between the island's tendency to manifest from the minds of the castaways and the many pseudo-Buddhist and Hindu winks from the Dharma Initiative.

Ben's dubious "magic box" is hardly the first in the show. Many have frustratingly pointed out that *Lost* is a "magic box" within another "magic box" within another, and another. A matryoshka nesting doll of a plot. The island itself was a magic box; the plane, the caves, the hatch, even the characters led lives that were full of unknowns — more magic boxes.

The writers' fascination with the idea of a magic box is not the only reason for *Lost*'s popularity though. There are certainly many other ingredients in the *Lost* formula that have a persistent impact on its success. At the core of this may be the island itself.

>: "The art of the tease is what this show is all about, nfound… As long as we can eventually deliver. And with all your love, faith and fanditude (not a word), I believe we can."
— Damon Lindelof, 2/18/05

>: "THE STAND totally inspired LOST — Good vs. Evil. Huge ensemble cast. Shades of the supernatural. And some of the best character work in a piece of popular fiction that I have ever read. Charlie was actually modeled after Larry Underwood in some ways… minus the heroin addiction (that I ripped off from Eddie Dean in the Dark Tower series)."
— Damon Lindelof, 11/25/04

>: "Watership [Down] happens to be one of my favorite books EVER, so I bent over backwards to get the publisher to clear it as a prop. Fiver's my favorite."
— Damon Lindelof, 11/4/04

Joseph Campbell was a self professed mythographer, who spent his career as a lecturer and writer revealing his findings through thousands upon thousands of comparative myth studies. During the course of his work, Campbell picked

The Hero's Journey

Joseph Campbell's studies on how mythology interfaces with the human psyche have resulted in numerous clinical applications, but his greatest contribution is without question to the world of entertainment. His theory of the "hero's journey" has gone from being a template to explain our fascination with folktales, to a template for creating new stories. Some of the points of the "hero's journey" that seem relevant to the construction of *Lost* are:

1. **Call to adventure:** Sometimes a call, sometimes a stumbling-upon; either way, the hero finds himself at the threshold of a great quest in a mysterious land. (The fuselage survivors, reeling from their unlikely survival, stand on the beach in wonder as a mysterious beast thrashes through the jungle. The next day, the heroes must decide if they will brave the beast to retrieve the plane's transponder.)

2. **Refusal of the call:** The hero is tempted to ignore his calling and return to his previous life. (Sort of explains many of the characters, but particularly the contrast between Jack and Locke. Jack seeks to bring everyone home; Locke feels their destiny is on the island.)

3. **Supernatural aid:** Once committed to the journey, a magical being arrives to assist the hero(es). (Arguably, this could be Ben, or any number of the ghostly apparitions that exist within *Lost*.)

4. **Crossing the threshold:** Now that the hero has answered the call, they find themselves having to let go of their previous worldview. Campbell describes the hero sometimes encountering a "threshold guardian" at this point. (The Dharma Initiative?)

5. **Return to the ordinary world:** Having survived whatever trials await in the special world, the hero now returns to the normal world. (In the case of *Lost*, this may not necessarily be the Oceanic 6, since it appears that their quest is not over, but Campbell observed that the return trip may not be entirely successful the first time around.)

6. **Applying the boon:** The hero returns from the special world with powers that are beneficial to all mankind. (The cure for cancer, anyone?)

up on a phrase coined by fellow literary junkie, and prolific novelist, James Joyce: monomyth. Joyce had written a novel named *Finnegans Wake* and had coined the term to express a singularity of storytelling style. It was Campbell who would express the more common definition of the term

J.J. Abrams is all smiles — no wonder since he knows all the secrets of *Lost*.

as a sort of template for the great hero myths. Campbell managed to distill the character types and situations down to particular archetypes. Strip away the genders, settings and names, and you would have situations and personalities that seem to always evoke the same sort of responses.

Campbell's work was heavily influenced by psychologist Carl Jung, most widely known for his work on the concept of a collective unconscious. Jung sought to understand the human condition by cracking the code of symbolism in dreams, myths and religion. Jung's approach was far more nebulous than Campbell's own work, which was more concerned with deciphering the appeal of certain forms of literature. Campbell found, in his comparing of thousands of myths, that a certain common structure existed: a "hero's journey." Each journey could be broken down to a series of stages. Could *Lost*'s basis be found there as well?

Castaway stories are a genre of their own. The "stranded on a deserted island" motif, which offers the castaway redemption through involuntary isolation, exists as a "station" in hero stories as far back as Jonah, Jason and the Argonauts, and even Gilgamesh himself. The first popular fictional castaway story was Defoe's *Robinson Crusoe*.

Not all analysts of *Lost* are quick to dismiss the castaway genre as being important to understanding the show's success, but to some the notion that the mere base of the plot — castaways surviving in a strange and wondrous location — is the essence of *Lost*'s success is ludicrous. Think about this: *Robinson Crusoe* is considered to be the Gilgamesh of the English language. This is not to say they are the same story, mind you. *The Epic of Gilgamesh*, from Ancient Mesopotamia, is a far more fanciful tale. Regarded as the earliest known work of literary fiction, the poem tells of King Gilgamesh's search for inner redemption by embarking on several heroic quests. One character in *Gilgamesh*, Endiku, is thought to have been parlayed into the character of Mr. Eko, with Locke being the Gilgamesh of season 2. While literary history is constantly in revision, it is generally accepted that *Robinson Crusoe* was the first novel to be written in English, and since its publication the novel has consistently been one of the most often reprinted works of fiction in circulation. Crusoe's tale of 28 years on a deserted island has become as close to a modern-age, enduring myth as any other in our culture.

So, audiences like a mystery box; we are predisposed to respond to certain characters and events; and our literary past shows an undeniable attraction to tales of characters abandoned on strange and forbidding islands, fighting for survival, redemption and existential peace. But what about *Lost* as a pure myth in its own right?

The story arc of the Dharma Initiative brought to *Lost* several modern archetypes. The hatch was a powerful symbol of revelation. Underworld settings are a common feature of monomythic epics. In the most latent sense, they represent the "other side." It could be said that the hatch promised the "higher truth" of the island. In a lot of ways, this idea has proven to be correct.

If we rewind to the sensibilities of 1977, when *Star Wars* first hit screens, the Cold War had created the image of the grey, mechanized façade of the Soviet Union. In our caricaturized view of soviet life, they all dressed alike, were godless and were bent on our destruction. Consider the Death Star now: it is the underworld of *Star Wars: A New Hope*. Inside the beast (arguably the belly of the whale but certainly as close to an underworld archetype as Lucas took the mythology at that point), we found a civilization of grey-and-white beings. Insanely uniform, mechanized and bent on destroying freedom lovers everywhere.

In *Lost*'s underworld we find the remnants of an idealist culture fallen victim, apparently, to its own technology. Desmond's mission of entering the numbers every 108 minutes on faith alone could be the writers speaking to our own anxieties about how our reliance on technology has enslaved us. The odd combination of a derelict technological age (8-bit computers, lava lamps and turntables) brought to bear on a purpose that seems futuristic could be seen as an expression of the dizzying speed of technological achievement — perhaps a woeful look back at all that could have been accomplished but wasn't, the cry of a forgotten technological age trying to reassert its failed utopian promises and stay relevant in our memories. Or, just cool anachronistic art direction.

For all of its magical boxes, ancient mythological overtones and pop culture winks, *Lost* clearly comes across as a mythmaker, as well as a mirror on many great myths. It speaks to us from some place we can't quite put a finger on, yet we know so well.

Chapter 5

THE HATCH
THAT ROARED

AS CONNECTED TO THE FANBASE as the creative team behind *Lost* has
been, said fanbase still surprises them from time to time. One of the biggest
surprises came after the season 1 finale. The second half of the season had
steadily been building up to what was sure to be an explosive ending. Much of
the focus was on two burgeoning storylines: Locke's obsession with the hatch,
and the launching of Michael's raft. In the finale, the raft set off, as anticipated,
but the story took a shocking twist — the Others abducted Walt! — and the
audience loved it. As for the hatch story, the big surprise for the audience was
that the hatch was finally opened — but we did not get to see what was inside.
It was like unwrapping a gift, then not being allowed to pull the lid off the box.
For a vocal portion of the fanbase, it was a huge letdown, and the resulting
uproar from those fans was an eye-opener for the creators.

Plotting a show as complex as *Lost* is obviously not an easy task. That
they would try to end the phenomenal first season in a memorable way was
a given. The writing team had carefully constructed their debut season with
various plot "tent poles" that had to be reached by the finale. The story of the
raft being built, burned and rebuilt came to the assumed culmination of it

finally being launched — but the writers threw in the unexpected twist of Walt being taken. It was a great setup and the audience bought into it: hook, line and sinker.

The other storyline that had been barreling towards some sort of resolution in the finale revolved around the mysterious hatch. Though the focus was more on Locke's obsession with opening it than on the hatch itself (to Boone's peril) there was an assumption by many viewers that we would discover whatever secret lurked inside it in the finale — a subtle but intriguing nugget to meditate on between seasons. The creators knew there was a high level of interest in the hatch, but they believed that the revelation of its contents could be deferred until the season 2 premiere. Jack, Locke, Kate and Hurley managed to open the hatch, but that was as far as it went. End of episode, end of season. But the beast that they had created and allowed to rile up the audience came back to bite them in their collective asses when the fans went nuts over yet another "unanswered question" — in fact, it was an answer they had been led to believe they would be getting.

The hiatus between seasons 1 and 2 became the "What's in the hatch?" summer. Every interview with anyone on or affiliated with the show included that same question. It was *Lost*'s version of "Who shot J.R.?" The outcry from the fans, especially the online ones, was so loud that the regular media outlets (who for a long time ignored the existence of online fandoms) could not help but take notice. By Comic Con in July 2005, it was not just the fans bombarding the *Lost* contingent with "What's in the hatch?", but every reporter as well. At the *Lost* season 1 DVD launch party held in Hawaii at the end of the summer in 2005, Damon Lindelof acknowledged the fans' frustration, but suggested that the season 2 premiere should make up for that. In his words, "Had we ended the season with what happens immediately after the hatch-opening, the fans would have been far more frustrated."

This intense level of scrutiny by fans and the media magnified the pressure on *Lost* Labs tenfold. Not only did they need to reveal the contents of the hatch as soon as possible, but they had to make it worth the extended wait. Luckily for *Lost* Labs, and the fans, the subsequent surfeit of theories that erupted after the discovery of Desmond and the Dharma Initiative was a hell of a twist. The general consensus from fans and critics alike was that the hatch contents more than lived up to the obscenely huge expectations. The uproar from fans that summer actually served to educate the creative team about their fanbase. They learned that fans are much more likely to forgive you if you make it worth their while. *Lost* Labs also learned not to make sweeping assumptions that the audience will "get" what is being portrayed on the screen.

The idea that the contents of the hatch would be revealed was a naïve assumption made by an audience still adapting itself to *Lost*'s cliffhanger modality. The "Perils of Pauline" concept of always leaving the viewer wondering what was next had been absent from television for some time, and the new breed of viewers who had come to watch *Lost* for its other trappings — beautiful cast, gorgeous locales, etc. — was not completely weaned away from the instant grati- fication of episodic TV. For those who still had not "gotten it," the idea that this is the way it was supposed to be was a bitter pill to swallow.

The discovery of the hatch, how- ever, was a tonal shift that seemed, curiously, to resonate from the view- er's side of the universe. Suddenly the fan community was awash with incredible speculation over what was

>: "Jenn: The finale should (read 'will') blow you away. Damon and Carlton (and the other writers) wrote perhaps the greatest final three hours of a series season EVER. It's IN-FRIGGIN-SANE."
— J.J. Abrams, 4/8/05

>: "Q, Sorry, but the questions are what make it fun. What gives the show to YOU guys. Seriously, is life NOT but a great mystery? I know there was a lot of unhappiness about waiting all summer to go in the hatch, but would you not have been even MORE frustrat[ed] if last week was the season finale (Jack/ Desmond meet) or worse yet, TONIGHT?? Do not fret. The end will come. It always does… "
— Damon Lindelof, 9/29/05

>: "Okay, loyalest of the loyal… I'm off to Carlton's to watch the Premiere with the rest of the writing gang. Hope you enjoy the episode and are feeling SOME degree of satisfaction for the LOOOOOONG wait."
— Damon Lindelof, 9/22/05

(All quotations from TheFuselage.com)

in the hatch, and the range of ideas was very telling. Some saw it as a door- way to another world, others imagined a room filled with computers stocked with detailed files on the crash survivors. Clones, zombies, aliens, a cockpit

The Dharma Initiative makes a comeback and starts recruiting
at San Diego Comic Con (July 2008).

for the island, secret labs, ghosts, a door to Central Park . . . , the range of ideas was vast, ludicrous and imaginative. What was it, though, about this nondescript hole in the ground that got people so excited?

Harold Perrineau was left screaming for *"Walt!"* in the ocean while his fellow Losties were peering into the hatch in the season 1 cliffhanger.

In the Jungian sense of the story, the hatch — an entry to the underworld — seems pregnant with answers, overdue answers at that. The underworld is considered to be, among other things, a locus of mystery, and the spiritual home of either good or evil. It is also often referred to as the dream realm. In nearly every culture, tales that involve a descent into the underworld end in the hero's rebirth as a man of purpose. For fans wrangling with the show's oblique mythology, which was never as impenetrable as it was during season 1, passage into the hatch — the underworld of *Lost* — seemed to promise the answers to everything.

During the days leading up to the finale, speculation over what was inside the hatch illuminated the seemingly endless imagination of the viewers. Some saw it as spiritual device. To them, the hatch could be the doorway to another world, a veritable "Stairway to Heaven," or the threshold to the next great stage of the adventure, stripping the story of the confines of the island. Most fans agreed on more technologically rooted theories, and many of those theories came true in a strange, roundabout way: a time machine; a control room for the island; the source of the island's healing power. More drab possibilities included a bank of computers, each containing detailed files on the survivors of the crash. Each speculation held a mirror to the speculator, likely revealing what each of us saw in our own underworld. For instance, one intrepid blogger (who shall remain nameless) said that when Locke opened the hatch he would be confronted by a well-dressed version of himself. Locke would stammer out "Oh my . . . ," and his duplicate would finish his sentence for him: "God? Not yet."

Identifying the reason for the fans' disappointment in the lack of a definitive hatch reveal isn't an easy task, but as the seasons have progressed, whatever
force drives it has certainly not gone away. The simplest explanation is that
for all the work the fanbase went through trying to predict the contents of the
hatch, they were left with a summer-long wait to settle their bets. However, the
writers are generally farther ahead than viewers give them credit for. Carlton
Cuse summarized this by saying, "The assumption that you can figure it all out
presupposes that you know enough about the world of the show to figure it all
out. If I were to ask you towards the end of season 1 what your theory on what
all the revelations of *Lost* are, you're going to give a wildly different answer than
you would now part way through season 4."

It seems that when huge reveals are forecast, there is competition in the
fandom to be the first to correctly predict the answer. The mass speculation
brings out the most creative of the base, and before you know it you have the
spirit of Dionysus sitting next to every *Lost* fan who has a forum account.

Every season since the season 1 finale has had a similar "hatch gate"
moment — a time where the fans generate so many incredibly imaginative pre-
dictions in response to a major event or reveal that the final resolution seems
mundane. For season 2, the event was clearly the revelation of the reason for
the crash of Oceanic 815. Again fans ran the gambit of speculations from ludicrous to ingenious; and again, once the episode aired, there was an almost
immediate backlash that the Swan Station's electromagnetic misfire bringing
the plane down was too telegraphed.

The argument that the fans are more imaginative than the writers of *Lost*
is a moot argument. It is based on the comparison of thousands of idea-gener-
ating diehards with a small but mighty creative team. For all of the finely honed
concepts created by fans though, none have yet presupposed the complex
mosaic of *Lost*. Our victories are limited to occasionally out-creating the writers,
but never achieving the full clarity of the Writers' Room's magic frequency.
But even if we do get it right, we won't know until proof has come to pass.
"Occasionally people do stumble upon bits and pieces of things that are true
and I think that is great, but it has to remain *that* viewer's individual satisfaction because we're not going to ruin it for everybody else by saying 'Yes! That's
exactly what is going to happen,'" Cuse said when asked if fans had ever gotten
dangerously close to intuiting the answers to *Lost*'s mysteries.

The positive side effect of the tension between audience expectation and the *Lost* crew's output is that the end result is often more fantastic than anyone could have imagined. Although the writers failed to shine a light on the depths of the hatch in the season finale, the season 2 reveal of Desmond and the Dharma Initiative delivered to fans one of the most popular characters of the show, and offered a paradigm shift in the possible meaning of the island's mysteries that was worth the wait.

This *Lost* fandom that squawks so loudly when displeased has, in turn, according to executive producer Bryan Burk, helped the creative team determine whether or not the writers are "on point with their storytelling." For instance, in that same season finale, Walt was taken onto a boat full of people led by Mr. Friendly. The producers and writers knew that the people on the boat were the Others, but that revelation was not as clear to the viewing audience. As Burk explained it:

> . . . it was clear to us that it was the Others who took him [Walt]. However, [what] we realized afterwards from reading online was that people did not know that it was the Others. It was just a boat of people. So what we needed to do immediately was, at the beginning of season 2, was make it very, very clear that the people who took him were the Others. So in that respect, it helps us know whether or not things are working or not working or what's making sense.

Tapping into the Internet fanbase — not for contributions to the story, but for real fan feedback on what parts of the story they are "getting" or "not getting," which characters they are "feeling" or "not feeling" — has led to a kind of unwritten partnership between the fans and the creators of *Lost*. The fans have finally been able to communicate with the Writers' Room through more than just their demographics and Nielsen ratings.

Chapter 6

WHO'S FLYING THE PLANE?

DO YOU REMEMBER the first season of *Lost*? More specifically, do you remember the media surrounding the show during its freshman season? Do you remember who the mouthpiece for the show was? Of course you do — it was J.J. Abrams. He was the most well-known name attached to the show in the beginning, and he did the bulk of the press. J.J. is more than just a genius, he's a hell of a salesman. He is cool as a cucumber in a room full of press people — he knows what to comment on, what not to comment on and what to be intentionally vague about. He is amazingly relaxed and gregarious in interviews, which leads to the interviewer falling under that J.J. spell, which in turn leads to yet another positive piece on that crazy new show called "Lost." With J.J. the extrovert handling the bulk of the sales pitches and question-answering during that first season, co-creator Damon Lindelof, the more introverted of the two, was able to focus on the Writers' Room and putting out scripts that would blow away an audience already voracious for this outside-the-box show.

As season 1 was coming to its explosive end, things at *Lost* Labs were rearranging. Abrams was preparing to direct the new *Mission: Impossible* movie, something that would occupy the bulk of his time for the next year. Lindelof

>: "Okay, folks, I'm out. It's amazing that I can write a show as intricate as LOST, but it takes me ten minutes to figure out how to post spoilers on the 'Lage. Man, I'm dumb."
— Damon Lindelof, 4/1/05

>: "Nighty-night all! Sorry can't hang longer, but you know… gotta put more eps in the ole' pipeline. That Monster is hungry and it needs to be fed! (disclaimer: 'The Monster' to which I refer is in fact abc and not The Monster Monster which will remain clouded in mystery until I bloody well see fit.)"
— Damon Lindelof, 2/18/05

was being pushed more and more into the limelight, without Abrams as a buffer, and expectations for the show continued to escalate as well. J.J. had created or co-created two previous television shows (*Felicity* and *Alias*) and he'd handled the various aspects of being a showrunner, as well as writing and directing. For Damon Lindelof, this was his first foray into leading a show, and he did not have the benefit of a smaller show and smaller network to get his feet wet as Abrams did. This was a case of being dropped into the deep end of the swimming pool — full of sharks — and being told to swim and fight for your life.

And yet . . . Damon Lindelof pulled through it, relatively unscathed, at least in the eyes of the public. The transition was a tricky one, though. The most important thing that Damon had to do was make the show *his*, not J.J.'s. He needed people on staff that *he* worked well with and who *he* could trust — something that J.J. is notorious for, too. The person he turned to was his former boss from when he was on staff at *Nash Bridges*, Carlton Cuse. Cuse not only was someone Lindelof knew he worked well with, but he was also someone with many more years of experience in the business — most importantly, he had experience as a showrunner. Lindelof needed someone next to him who he could trust implicitly, and who would trust him right back. Carlton Cuse was, and still is, that person.

Finding someone to run *Lost* with him was just the beginning for Damon Lindelof. As the first season progressed, dissension began to develop in the

Writers' Room, most of it in the form of co-executive producer David Fury. As with most stories, there are two sides to the tale of why Fury left after season 1. In this case, Fury chose to talk openly to *Rolling Stone* magazine about *Lost*'s "master plan":

> "There was absolutely no master plan on *Lost*," insists David Fury . . . "anybody who said that was lying. . . . They keep saying there's meaning in everything, and I'm here to tell you no — a lot of things are just arbitrary."

Fury's greatest crime wasn't that he dismissed the infamous "road map" for *Lost* that executive producers Damon Lindelof, Carlton Cuse and Bryan Burk have all insisted exists, or even that he chose to leave the show. It was that he burned a bridge and did it in a very public way. Hollywood has a long memory, while most television shows have a relatively short shelflife. It is unusual for a writer in that industry to publicly criticize his former showrunners/coworkers, potentially harming his chances of working for or with them again in the future.

More changes came after Fury's vocal departure: during seasons 2 and 3 there appeared to be a revolving door on the *Lost* Writers' Room. Casual viewers may not have noticed the ever-changing names that flashed across the screen at the beginning of each episode, but for the contingent of fans who are steeped in *Lost* and who regularly pick apart episodes, the changes were very evident. One of the more brilliant additions to *Lost* Labs came in the form of script coordinator Gregg Nations. Nations was brought

>: "…this was the first official writing effort by Carlton Cuse, the rarely mentioned but absolutely KEY Executive Producer who joined our merry band right after the writing of 'Solitary.' I wish I could take credit for tonite's Ep, but I was actually away for the week it was penned… so other than some story work prior to my escape, Carlton stepped up and brought this baby home in a major way. He's a guy who likes to stay behind the scenes and isn't much for tooting his own horn (thus his absence on our blessed Fuselage), but I just want you all to know what a huge part of the show he is."
— Damon Lindelof, 1/13/05

(All quotations from TheFuselage.com)

in at the end of season 1 to handle continuity, organize that element of the show and then hold on tight. To fill such a vital position, Damon Lindelof and Carlton Cuse again chose someone they knew — Gregg had also been a part of *Nash Bridges*. Considering the huge main cast and multiple storylines, both in the past and the present, Nations had to develop a tracking system for all of the details, no matter how big or small, and he has handled the monumental task with amazing dedication and aplomb.

Damon takes over the mic from J.J., much like he had to take over running the show as J.J. got involved in other projects.

With Carlton Cuse as his copilot and Gregg Nations on board to handle the continuity, Damon Lindelof was in a more secure position as *Lost*'s co-creator/showrunner/writer. One obvious indication that the team of Damon and Carlton, known as "Darlton" on the boards, had fully taken the reins of the show was the number of interviews and soundbites, from one or both of them, that ramped up that summer between seasons 1 and 2, and led into season 2, with the first "official" podcasts. The podcasts, starring Darlton, had a mixed effect on the *Lost* fandom when they began: on one hand, Damon and Carlton were directly addressing questions asked by fans and helping to quash various rumors as they arose, and that was received as a good thing. On the other hand, Darlton's combined knack for sarcasm and sometimes caustic wit rubbed some fans the wrong way. Who wants to send in a question to the showrunners of their favorite show, only to have their chosen screenname, number of posts and sometimes the question itself mocked? Anyone familiar with Lindelof and Cuse's repartee knew that it was simply their kind of humor — but to fans who were less familiar with these guys and their humor, the snarkiness seemed to cross the line at times.

Thankfully, someone — most likely from ABC's public relations department — knocked a little sense into the Darlton duo, and they began sounding more PR-friendly, though there are still glimmers of that fiendish wit lacing their comments. In fact, by season 3 it seemed as if Damon, Carlton and the rest of the producers had all been given some kind of PR guidebook. Questions from the media were given the same regurgitated answers, regardless of who was being interviewed. The *Lost* Labs' group had not only become more media savvy, they had taken some form of control over what was said to the media — period.

The most extreme example of this "controlled media" initiative was directed at three of the most well-known television columnists/reporters: Kristin Veitch (nka Kristin Dos Santos, from E!), Michael Ausiello (from *TV Guide*) and Jeff Jensen (from *Entertainment Weekly*). It seemed like a good enough plan. Lindelof and Cuse offered up, well . . . themselves, on a silver platter, via exclusive interviews, wherein they might offer up some harmless spoilers. In exchange, these reporters would keep a lid on any explosive spoilers that might come across their desks or e-mail accounts. Sounds like a smart plan, right? Well, there was one giant flaw in this scheme — the *Lost* fans figured it out very early on, which reduced the online "street cred" of those three reporters. The fans knew that they were only giving out "Darlton-approved" information, and knowing how much Damon Lindelof hates spoilers, we knew those guys were never going to give out anything juicy. The reporters were viewed as Darlton mouthpieces — which really tainted both sides for a while.

Jeff Jensen took things one step further down the road to (potential) disaster during the infamous "radio silence" that Darlton had created weeks away from the season 3 finale, and that continued until the season 4 premiere — a *very* long nine months later. At one point, Jensen declared in his *Entertainment Weekly* column that he was going to scour the *Lost* theories and "burning questions" out in the fandom and each week have Damon or Carlton directly address them. The problem with this seemingly sound idea is that as much as *Lost* fans may seem to complain about all the unanswered questions — there are few who actually want *everything* answered, at least, not outside the show itself, and definitely not in the pages of a magazine! As for the theories, yes, there are some humdingers out there, but part of the beauty of the show is that it drives us to come up with these bizarre explanations that have just a sliver of plausibility. To present these to Darlton and have them shot down one by one would have crushed the spirit of the theorists — not a very productive idea considering that theories and rumors were the only things keeping the *Lost* conversation alive during the horrifically long hiatus.

The journey for *Lost*'s showrunners from season 1 onward has not been a very linear or smooth one, to say the least. Each new season has been approached in a new and different way with respect to what would be revealed to the media and when, with sometimes contradictory reveals. But when "radio silence" was instituted again a few weeks before the season 4 finale, Darlton and *Lost* Labs appeared to have established their *modus operandi* for handling the all-important information machine. With the announcement that *Lost* would end in 2010, no doubt remained about who was flying the plane towards the culmination of this behemoth of a show.

PART 2

Chapter 7

FROM THE WATERCOOLER TO THE OCEAN

IT IS IMPOSSIBLE TO TALK about the *Lost* fandom, especially the online contingent, without including the group of bloggers and fans whose names have become almost as synonymous with *Lost* as those of Damon Lindelof and Carlton Cuse. The complexity and proliferation of mysteries in *Lost* have attracted a special breed of fan equipped with above-average intelligence and a burning desire to debate. The fans' need for information from and in-depth discussions with people of equal or higher intelligence resulted in an outpouring of blogs and forums dedicated to picking apart the plot of *Lost* as it unfolds. The entertainment value of the show is the same as other prime-time dramas — but the sophistication and unpredictability of the episodes have made it rise above typical television fare, and it offers an ethos that goes far beyond anything else on television.

Initially, the complex nature of the *Lost* story stunned audiences. While the overall success of the show is certainly the result of a massive "X factor," the nebulous nature of the imagery and plot devices, and the oblique narrative probably brought as many fans to the Internet seeking answers as it did those seeking to discuss those very elements on an academic level.

The fans' hunger for information paved the way for many superstars to emerge within the world of the Internet; at the same time, the demand for accurate information presented in an interesting way set the bar high for anybody daring enough to call themselves an "expert" on *Lost*.

Some of the earliest "experts" emerged, naturally, on the pages of The Fuselage. Other personalities, such as DarkUFO, got their start on other, more generalized boards. DarkUFO, or Andy, was well known for compiling spoilers on IMDb.com (Internet Movie Database) long before he launched his own website, with an interim gig as webmaster of The Tail Section's spoiler blog.

One of the earliest blogs to become a must-read was Ben Sledge's (yes, that is his real name) "Sledgeweb's Lost Stuff." Sledgeweb's approach treated each episode as an "investigation," and Sledge's propensity for detail made him the most thorough Easter egg hunter in the business. To this day, Sledgeweb is the yardstick for examining, cross-referencing, interpreting and explaining the various bits of minutiae hidden within each episode.

Carlton Cuse, Damon Lindelof and surprise guest Matthew Fox
answer questions during the *Lost* panel at Comic Con (July 2008).

Dark∪ғᴏ emerged as the electronic equivalent of a news-clipping agency. Hosting a mass of sharp-minded contributors who provide original content, Dark∪ғᴏ's site is perhaps best known as the nexus of everything that is *Lost* in the mass media. Testing the bounds of "fair use," the blog has become a gathering point for even the most offhand mentions of *Lost* in the mass media. If *Entertainment Weekly* publishes an article on *Lost*, you can be sure it will be cut, copied and pasted into the appropriate category on Dark∪ғᴏ's sprawling network of *Lost* blogs.

Blogs are just the beginning, though. For Hawaiian husband-and-wife team Jen and Ryan Ozawa of "The Transmission" (www.hawaiiup.com/lost), podcasting has been raised to state of the art. Preceding the inception of the official *Lost* podcast, "The Transmission" dominated the iTunes scene with its "on location" reports and in-depth examinations.

"The Transmission" was joined by one of the most successful single ventures in *Lost* podcasting, the Jay & Jack podcast (www.jayandjack.com).Jay and his stepfather Jack were already ardent fans of the show, but Jay's penchant for music and recording would lure them to express their fandom on the audio spectrum. "Jack and I talked about the show and theorized about the show so much, and I had wanted to do some kind of podcast and it clicked that a podcast where we talked about *Lost* would work," Jay told DocArzt, recounting how it all got started.

Eventually, "The Transmission" went on a long hiatus, during which time Ryan joined the Jay & Jack team to provide spoiler and filming updates from the island. At one point, much to Jay & Jack's amazement, another luminary from the *Lost* world stopped by the show. "Jorge [Garcia] called us after our sixth episode. We were still very new and crappy and didn't believe it at first. But I heard it and got Jack to listen; then, that whole day, I told everyone that Jorge Garcia called the show. And I thought to myself it doesn't get any better than that."

In the time since that call, Jorge has joined Jay & Jack on the air not only for the *Lost* podcast, but also for a special benefit podcast for autism. Such meldings of the "official" world with those on the blog fringe are not so common outside of The Fuselage.

One of the most impressive sites on the web belongs, really, to the fan community itself. Lostpedia.com launched as a small project and quickly attracted a large influx of editors. Relying on the same reader-generated content as Wikipedia does, and running the same platform, it is a searchable online encyclopedia in which the contributions of the myriad of visitors combine to make Lostpedia an unmatched resource for *Lost* researchers.

During The Lost Experience alternate reality game (ARG), the ABC network chose to emulate the successes of the fan scene by creating several blogs to follow the exploits of a girl named Rachel Blake. Each country had its own persona. In the U.S. it was the silhouetted form of a guy named Speaker (Andy Floyd), wearing white sunglasses. In Australia it was The Lost Ninja (Tom Ragg). Both correctly conveyed the sensibilities of the *Lost* blog scene because, well, they were both bona fide *Lost* geeks with a tireless lust for the chase. These two bloggers were always kept slightly more informed than the public, and along with counterparts from other nations, they were easily accepted by the grass roots scene as "the real deal" . . . because they were.

Tom Ragg reminisced about the experience with great fondness:

"Working on TLE was one of the most satisfying working experiences of my entire life, as well as the most consuming. Over the course of the five-month span, an amazing community came together, most of which still stands strong today. While the actual gameplay components were great, it was definitely the fanbase and community that made the event. I found myself setting up mics around my spare room so that I could DJ for fifty-strong chatrooms, talking about where to find the next eight-second video clue. I spent hours arranging five thousand chocolates to be given free from comic book stores, an act that got me huge kudos but turned me off chocolate for the rest of time. Most of all, I loved leading a community based around one of my passions and making many, many new friends that I still keep close contact with today."

The end of a *Lost* episode on television is far from the end of the episode online. Considering the large primary cast, it is surprising that the audience can connect to the show on a weekly basis, but they do. The office watercooler talk the morning after doesn't revolve strictly around plot developments, but rather leans towards deeper discussions centered on philosophy, religion and the nature of humanity. The simpler questions, such as "Who is Jacob?" and "Who fathered Sun's baby?" are just minor details compared to the cacophony of follow-up questions to those inquiries. We don't just ask, "Who is Jacob?" — we ask: What does he want? Why can only certain people see him and his cabin? Is Ben being manipulated by him or is Jacob actually the one being manipulated? Did he really say "Help me!" to Locke? If so, is helping Jacob part of Locke's destiny? Whenever answers arrive, they quickly lead to more questions, and layer-by-layer, more answers are revealed . . . only to lead to even *more* questions.

>: "Arabchick — I was raised by wolves. My mother cared only for a warm cave to lay her head, the meat of a fresh kill and the well-being of her cubs (and me). She never got around to teaching me the value of not teasing."
— Damon Lindelof, 2/18/05

>: "dia — well, I am not at liberty to discuss which eppy it is just yet, but let's just say that a lot of questions will be answered… and a lot of answers will be questioned!"

— Javier Grillo-Marxuach, 7/13/05
>: "All about — well, as hot as they let us get away [with] in primetime. There will definitely be some shirtless Locke today."
— Javier Grillo-Marxuach, 10/5/05

The density of the plot guarantees that viewers will never have all the answers, which could be disheartening for some fans of the show. And yet, it works most of the time. It allows us to pick the show apart and invent our own theories about what we know and don't know. Those same fans parlay their theories online, read other fantastical theories and jump right into heated debates over who is right . . . if anyone. The tapestry of *Lost* is so thick and lush that there always seems to be someone who has dug deeper than you did or noticed a hidden Easter egg that you did not see. The show seems to have boundless possibilities.

Something else that inflames this desire to theorize and participate in heated discussion is the interconnecting backstories of the survivors of Oceanic Flight 815. Call them Easter eggs or blame the concept of "six degrees of separation" — either way, this intentional overlapping of characters in the flashbacks sparks a fan's need to find a compatriot somewhere, anywhere — at home, at work or online — to scream "Did you *see* that? Locke was checking the meter at Nadia's house. And she's Sayid's lost love!!!" or "Did you *hear* that? Hurley owns a box company. Didn't Locke work for a box company?" *Lost* is attractive to those who thrive on analyzing, debating and conjecturing.

In the context of such an incredibly smart fandom, anyone who is consistently brilliant in theorizing and finding the hidden clues and connections eventually ends up with a following of his or her own. My (that is, DocArzt's) first site, The Tail Section (www.thetailsection.com), was an early fan favorite. *Lost* became more than just a show I liked to blog about, it became my job and a huge part of my life. A handful of *Lost* bloggers have gained their own level of celebrity within the fandom — even to the point of getting noticed by "real" media outlets and people within *Lost* Labs itself. As so many people have said, the Internet has made the world a smaller place. If I did not have the Internet as an outlet for my island ramblings, I might have gotten some articles published in a magazine or local newspaper. Without a recognizable name as a reporter or writer, any celebrity I might have reached from those writings probably would have remained local.

But we *do* have the Internet and sites like The Tail Section have attracted their own fans within the fandom. *Lost* fans were flocking to these independent blogs and discussion forums, rather than waste their time on regular entertainment and news sites that were not bothering to find true *Lost* fans to write episode reviews. *Entertainment Weekly* was one of the first traditional media outlets to identify the *Lost* fans as a group that would not fall for the same old dog and pony show when it came to reviewing the episodes. Whether it was a stroke of luck or calculated genius, *EW*'s Jeff Jensen (also called "Doc Jensen") jumped into the *Lost* fandom wielding a blogger's sensibility of what his target audience — the rabid *Lost* fans with insatiable appetites — wanted to read. And he gave it to them (and still gives it to them).

Media outlets were not the only ones who became aware of the burgeoning *Lost* fandom's need for information and discussion: Damon Lindelof, Carlton Cuse and ABC took notice as well. Damon and Carlton began to do their own "official" podcasts for the show, seemingly to help quash rumors and answer fan questions, but also to tap into the mass appeal of fan podcasts, like the extremely popular The Lost Podcast With Jay & Jack. ABC, being the network conglomerate it is, understood that these podcasts were taking fans away from their own site. ABC showed their recognition of the savviness of the Lost fans by employing Lost fans to blog and help give out clues during the two ARGS: The Lost Experience and Find 815 (see page 131). Speaker and The Lost Ninja were a large part of the success

Jay (on the right) and Jack (in the middle) are interviewed by TV.com after catching a preview screening of Bad Robot's next TV project, *Fringe*, at Comic Con. Their *Lost* podcast is one of the most popular fan-made podcasts on iTunes.

of those ARGS. They were obviously fans first, so they knew what would interest and entice other fans. If ABC had gone in-house for people to handle the blogs and clues, the super-aware Lost fans would have eviscerated the "n00bs" (see Appendix).

The efficiency of the clue-solving militia has evolved to such an extent that it is nearly impossible for the writers and producers of *Lost* to put anything on screen that will remain unexamined. A classic example is the blast-door map from the season 2 episode "Lockdown." In this episode, John Locke is pinned down by a blast door when the Swan Station goes into "lockdown." It was later revealed that the purpose of the lockdown may have been the delivery of a Dharma resupply pallet that was parachuted into the jungle nearby. The lockdown itself delivered a chunk of mythology both to John Locke and fans alike that continues to inform to this day. On the back of the blast-door, visible only in the rays of the ultraviolet emergency lights spectrum, was a map of the Dharma facilities on the island.

Appearing onscreen only for a few moments, the elaborate map was both a diagram of the locations of key Dharma facilities and a cryptic diary composed of mathematical formulas, Latin phrases and various enigmatic statements. At first blush, this glimpse seemed like something that would take fans days, perhaps weeks, to decode. In fact, it took less than nine hours.

For the fansites that took part in disseminating the information, the blast door was also a wake-up call. In the days that followed the successful decoding of the map, practically every major *Lost* fansite and forum suffered some degree of traffic-induced shutdown. The demand for answers on this pivotal piece of mythology had reached server-melting proportions.

The argument could be made that the quest for watercooler talking points has surpassed the need for simple enjoyment of the show. Many of *Lost*'s most diehard online theorists are frequently positing overly complicated scenarios for what is "really" going on with the show — everything from multidisciplinary time-space theories that attempt to validate the pseudoscience of the show, to various theories tied to the myriad literary references in the show.

When Carlton Cuse and Damon Lindelof were asked if anyone had come so close to solving the show that they felt drastic measures would be called for (i.e., lying), Cuse responded that there was still a lot to be learned before fans could hope to get it right. "What we would say is there are still twists and turns and unexpected surprises to come, so it's really hard to figure out where we're going because the audience doesn't possess enough information yet," and even if they had been lucky enough to piece together a significant nugget of truth and wanted confirmation, the halls of *Lost* Labs would be unyielding

According to "Darlton," it is not really possible at this point in the show's unfolding for any fan to come up with a theory that accurately explains everything, due to the fact that there are still major reveals ahead that the showrunners claim will take the story in unexpected directions. Should learning that cause the hardcore theorists to give up? Most definitely not. Again, a part of the beauty of the show is that the intentional lack of black-and-white answers to all of the mysteries guarantees that *Lost* fans will *always* have a wide variety of theories to test out, and each has the potential to be correct to some degree. It is impossible for any true theorist to become bored while watching this show. The *Lost* writers are only releasing as much information as they are ready for the audience to see at this point, but there are also clues scattered amongst the chaff. Going back to rewatch the first and second season episodes proves that the clues are there — if you know what you are looking for.

The plethora of forums catering to *Lost* theorists — and the famed *Lost* bloggers who pick apart each episode for their readers, then discuss them heartily in the comment sections, sometimes racking up hundreds of comments for one episode recap — are in no danger of running out of material to test the existing theories or to cultivate new ones. Even as the answers to some of the long-standing mysteries begin to be revealed as the show barrels towards its series finale, each new answer still leads to many more questions. The watercooler crowd is not in any danger of abandoning their *Lost* talk anytime soon.

Chapter 8

BREAKING DOWN THE WALL – ONE FAN'S EXPERIENCE

By hijinx

BEFORE *LOST*, I had never owned a domain name, designed or maintained a website, started or even joined a fan club for anyone. This show, or more specifically the people behind the show, changed all of that. Of course, I feel like I should stamp a big, red sign at the beginning of this chapter that says: "Results not typical." As time has passed, I have become increasingly aware of just how true that statement is when it comes to my experiences in the *Lost* fandom. So many factors were involved — a set of tumblers falling into just the right sequence at just the right time. It is not possible for me to write a dissertation on how to become an "insider fan" or a guidebook called "I was befriended by a Hollywood producer — Ask me how!" But relating the story of how I came to be in this unique position is something I don't mind sharing (at the very least because I know this chapter will cause Burky to squirm a bit).

It all started at The Fuselage, though that shouldn't be much of a shock. The unprecedented access to actors, writers and producers from *Lost* offered on The Fuselage has given *Lost* fans everywhere the opportunity to get to know these "VIPs" on a more human level, while in turn, those VIPs get to interact with their fans one on one. As we said in The Fuselage chapter (p. 19), the first year definitely saw the most VIP involvement, and I joined the site in mid-December 2004, about six weeks after the site went live. As part of my initial process of poking around the site to get a feel for it, I read the VIP Archive, which houses all of the posts made by VIPS on the linear board (the "LB"). Some VIP names I recognized, some I didn't. But either way, their posts were extremely entertaining.

One of the most active VIPS on the LB posted under the alias of "Burky." Reading through his posts, I figured out that Burky was the nickname for *Lost* executive producer Bryan Burk. He had a fantastic sense of humor, and I took a liking to him immediately. While looking around on the threaded portion (the "TB") of The Fuselage, I discovered that a fan group had been started for most of the other VIPS who were posting on The Fuselage, but I could not find anything for Burky. I was stunned, because it was obvious from his posts that he enjoyed getting to know the fans, and his posts were witty, informative and self-deprecating in the best possible way. There was no doubt in my mind that Bryan Burk should have his own fan group, so I started the "Burky Babes." At the time I started the group, I had no idea what he was actually responsible for at *Lost* Labs — I had never even interacted with him online yet. I just thought he was a really nice guy who deserved a fan group.

Javier Grillo-Marxuach, a supervising producer and writer for *Lost* during seasons 1 and 2, would later tell me that I "chose wisely." Looking back, knowing what I know now, it was an amazing stroke of luck; a "perfect storm" of circumstances that probably never would have converged in this way if I had harbored any underlying motives or actual intent to make it happen. It was the right person, the right show, the right time and the right fan. Four years later and this "insider fan" gig is still surrounded by an aura of surrealism for me.

The fan group came first, and was quickly followed by the website (www.bryanburk.com). The idea for the website actually came from J.J. Abrams. A Fuselager had asked Burky if he had a website; he said that he didn't and that only his mom would visit it if he did. Then J.J. (who had been lurking) popped on with the following statement: "I would visit bryanburk.com at least 100 times a day." My curiosity was peaked, so I checked to see if the domain was available — it was, so I bought it. I knew very little about Burky. I had never seen a picture of him, had no idea where he was from or even how old he was. All of that stuff was tertiary to the two main details I did know: (1) he worked on *Lost*;

and (2) he was incredibly nice to the fans on The Fuselage. I learned about his professional career as I researched stuff for the website (or "fansite" which is how we refer to a site that is made by a fan in honor of someone or something), but digging into the personal stuff has never been of any interest to me.

It didn't take long before Burky was linked to his fan group and then to the fansite. His posts on The Fuselage usually came in the middle of the night, a time when I was normally sleeping, so I had charged the other Babes to direct him to his fan group thread on the TB. He was extremely flattered, though somewhat embarrassed by all the attention directed at him. Burky is not the flashy guy in the limelight, so it was also decidedly weird for him — especially in the beginning. When I finally managed to be online one night at the same time that he was on, he had this to say to me about the fan group:

Hey, Hijinx — thanks for the creation of my absurd thread board! I am both humiliated, humbled and HUGELY flattered . . .

I guess I could have left it at that — the fan group thread on The Fuselage and the fansite. But I am not the type to do things half-assed. There came a time when Burky was absent from The Fuselage for a couple of weeks, which was unusual for him at that time. Some of us were worried by his absence, so we asked Damon Lindelof where Burky was the next time he was on. Damon said Burky was completely buried in work and that he "had not been home in two weeks, . . . was sleeping on a couch and had taken to muttering curses at people who walked by him on the Disney lot." Reading that led to my idea for the Babes to send Burky care packages to show him how much we appreciated his hard work and insane dedication to his job and the fans. Since it was my idea, I sent the first one out around the middle of February 2005. I am not sure what I actually thought Burky's reaction would be — I think I was mainly hoping that he wouldn't get mad at all the fuss. I kept checking the LB after I sent it, figuring that he would post there when he got the package. I definitely was not expecting the phone call I got about a week after the package went out. The man on the phone said he was Bryan Burk. I replied, "No, it's not!"

I was stunned. Even more surprising than the phone call itself was that Bryan had not even opened the package yet — he actually opened it and went through the contents while he was on the phone with me. Our conversation

hijinx is flanked by *Lost* executive producer Bryan Burk and surprise guest Greg Grunberg (who played the pilot of 815) at the first *Lost* fan party, known as Destination: LA 1, held in April 2005.

was sporadic in a hilarious way, because the man was doing no less than five things at once, all of which I was hearing on the phone as he periodically said, "Hold on a sec" . . . "Wait for two seconds" . . . "Hold on" . . . "Okay, I'm back . . . wait . . . hold another two seconds," and so on. I don't remember everything we talked about, but I know that I managed to remain relatively calm during the phone call itself, only to completely freak out the moment we hung up. That one phone call was a "gamechanger," the irony being that I was not aware that the game had changed at the time. As extremely cool as the call was, it would be another couple of months before I became aware of the extraordinary position the situation had put me in.

A few weeks after the phone call from Burky, I e-mailed him for the first time. I had received an e-mail via the fansite from someone he had gone to film school with at USC, so I forwarded it. Burky sent me a reply and e-mail has been our primary source of communication ever since. In the beginning, I only e-mailed him when I had something very specific to ask him or tell him. I did not want to be annoying or make him feel any sense of obligation to respond to me. The man had enough going on in his life without having to deal with a twittering fangirl on top of all that. He usually did respond, though, within a few days. Sometimes it took longer. Having no established precedent for exchanging e-mails with someone that far up the Hollywood food chain, I developed my own set of guidelines. Those rules have become more laid back as time has passed, but the underlying principle is: don't be a nuisance.

In April 2005, the first fan party for *Lost* — Destination: L.A. ("DLA1")

— took place. It was held at the Hollywood Highland Renaissance Hotel in Los Angeles, California. Before DLA1, I was already a huge fan of *Lost* and the people behind the show. After DLA1, I was a fan for life. This was not just due to the large VIP contingent, though it was admittedly pretty awesome to meet people like Damon Lindelof, J.J. Abrams and Daniel Dae Kim. What was practically unfathomable to me before I got to L.A. was that any VIP besides Burky and Javi would know who I was. So

>: "No, I'm not a writer (I can barely read, therefore, I produce)."
— Bryan Burk, 12/2/04

>: "The only person who would visit a 'bryanburk.com' would be my mom!"
— Bryan Burk, 12/16/04

>: "I would visit bryanburk.com at least 100 times a day."
— J.J. Abrams, 12/16/04

(All quotations from TheFuselage.com)

imagine my complete and utter shock as I was introducing myself to these people and, when they found out that I was the one responsible for Burky's fansite, they proceeded to tell me how much they loved the site or asked how to get a Babes T-shirt.

The first time it happened, I thought it was a fluke. Thom Sherman, who at the time was president of Bad Robot Productions, told me that he loved the site and in his autograph to me he wrote, "Thanks for all your support . . . of Burky!" I figured he was just flattered that I had recognized who he was and asked to have my picture taken with him. But then, I posed for a picture with Carlton Cuse, and afterwards he asked me, "Are you the one who does Burky's site?" I stuttered, "Uh, yeah." Then he said, "Well, how do I go about getting a Babes shirt?" Even with these early indications that word had traveled through both Bad Robot and *Lost* Labs about the fansite, *nothing* could have prepared me for what happened when I met J.J. Abrams. I had been talking to J.J.'s wife Katie while he was being mobbed in the hallway between the VIP Room and the Party Room. Katie somehow already knew about Burky showing up at Bowlapalooza the night before, so as we waited for J.J., I showed her and her friend pictures from my digital camera of the event. When J.J. got closer, Katie said to him, "J.J. come over here [waves him over to us]. You need to meet hijinx. She does the website for Bryan." As J.J. reaches out to shake my hand, he says to me, "Oh my gosh! That's you?" I nod. "You have made all of Bryan's

Bryan Burk, hijinx and William Mapother (Ethan Rom) catch up at
Destination: L.A. 2, held in May 2006.

In March 2007, hijinx had the chance to visit the offices of Bad Robot (then in Santa
Monica) with her friend q. Showing them around the place were Athena Wickham (far
left), Ben Sokolowski (second from right) and Dave Baronoff (far right).

wildest dreams come true!" Suddenly, Burky's comment when I was on the phone with him a couple of months before about some of his friends giving him a hard time about the site took on another meaning — he was referring to these guys, J.J., Katie, Thom, Carlton. These were the people who were picking on him.

Shortly after meeting J.J., I found Burky standing alone in the Party Room. He smiled over at me, so I walked up to him and said, "All of these people seem to know who I am and know that I run your website!" He chuckled and did not seem surprised by this revelation. I decided to take the opportunity to ask the "big question" for anyone who has ever made a fansite: "So, uh, can I be your 'official fansite'?" Another small laugh, then he said, "I thought you already were." I replied, "Well, I never actually *asked* you. . . ." Burky replied, "Well, I'm pretty sure yours is the only one out there anyway." I did not have a response for that, so I just thanked him. We talked about some other random things for a few minutes, then I decided to leave him be. I thanked him one more time, to which he responded, "No, thank *you*."

Living through the experience of DLA1 just once was more than enough to ensure my loyalty, to *Lost* and to Bad Robot, for many years to come. Little did I know that it was just the beginning.

Burky is not the only person inside *Lost* Labs or Bad Robot who I keep in contact with these days. After more than four years, I have gained quite a few e-mail addresses and phone numbers from the other side of that "wall." But I know without a doubt that these other people trust me because Burky trusted me first. His name carries a lot of weight — a lot more than I think even he realizes. I shudder to think of the consequences if someone with more nefarious purposes had registered his domain name instead of me. I have had one of the actors from the show and someone from ABC both tell me that their initial decision to reply to my inquiries was due to my e-mail address ending with "bryanburk.com." As well, I have "cyber-squatted" on a few other domain names in an effort to protect them from being used for malicious purposes — that is one area of vulnerability that Hollywood needs a serious education in.

For years I wondered why exactly Burky did trust me in the beginning. I had always felt he should have been more skeptical than he seemed to be. When I finally had the chance to ask him, his response was: "I didn't trust you." In fact, there was a point when it all became a little too weird for him and he was planning on calling to ask me to take the site down. But around that same time, I sent him an e-mail saying I had decided he should know more about who I am and why I made the fansite, and something in that e-mail made it click for him — he understood where I was coming from and saw that it was not a freakish place. As he put it, "I realized what you're excited about is not Bryan Burk. What you're excited about is . . . these worlds that we do and . . . being a part of it." I had explained in the e-mail how the shows he produced, *Lost* and *Alias*, were these great escapes for me and the fansite was a creative outlet for me to show my appreciation. He not only recognized that passion and excitement; he related to it. As Burky put it, "It's all about being part of something that is fun and different, and it's your world as much as it is ours — if not more so."

DLA1 was my first indication that my spontaneous decision to start Burky's fan group and make a fansite was going to result in much more than I had bargained for. Having this "official fansite," this e-mail address and this fairly well-known connection to Bryan Burk comes with a weight of responsibility as well. Anything I do, anything I say within the realm of the *Lost* fandom and the ever multiplying fandoms for Bad Robot's other projects, can reflect back on Burky. The power of that affiliation could easily be abused. I am extremely conscious of all the implications, which is something else that has endeared me to Burky. I have adopted what I can only think to call the Spiderman Creed: "With great power comes great responsibility." For every post I make, e-mail I send or interview I do, I view my response and my actions in the context of a "worst case scenario" — that being, what would Bryan think if this was sent to him?

That responsibility goes both ways. As fans recognize that I have a connection to Burky and others within *Lost* and Bad Robot, I try my best to seek answers to questions or help explain aspects of making the show whenever I can. In the same vein, I am well aware that sometimes I am the only direct and constant contact that Burky and the others have to the fans of their show. Representing a fandom can be a massive weight to bear, as well.

At the most recent *Lost* fan party (known as LOST Weekend), which was held in March 2007, I met Gregg Nations, script coordinator for *Lost* and an active contributor to The Fuselage. Since he only posts on the TB and I mainly stick to the LB, we had not really interacted before LOST Weekend. Afterwards, Gregg and I began e-mailing each other periodically. If I need a quick answer to a question from the fandom, Gregg is usually easier to get ahold of than Burky. I also sometimes share stories about the inner workings and politics of the *Lost* fandom with Gregg, stuff that doesn't typically come across his radar but that he is fascinated by. My unofficial title at The Fuselage is "Bad Robot Fan Liaison." It is a title that I made up, but which I think is a pretty accurate description for what I do within the *Lost* fandom.

Gregg and I have talked about this unique role that I stumbled upon, and he's told me that he thinks it is an important part of the fandom. He says, "It's good that someone has a foot in both the creative world and the fan world and understands the workings of both. Sometimes the two worlds are at odds, and the fan liaison translates back and forth." My greatest success from being in this position came when I was told by Gregg and a handful of other VIPs that interacting with me has helped them to have a better understanding of fans. Burky referred to me as being one of the "gatekeepers of *Lost* . . . a group of fans who have really taken a possession and a care of it." For me, it's not about having e-mail addresses and phone numbers for people like Gregg and Burky. It's about the show and this amazing fandom surrounding it. As "privileged" as I have been, if my work wasn't benefiting the *Lost* fandom as a whole, then it wouldn't be worth it to me.

Chapter 9

THE *LOST*
FAN PARTIES

THE FUSELAGE IS AS MUCH a social site as it is a fansite for *Lost*. Whether you favor the LB or a particular group of threads on the TB, you start recognizing other fans who post around the same time you do (on the LB) or in the same threads as you — and you start developing online friendships. The longer you have been there, the deeper those relationships can become . . . at least for those who aren't freaked out by the idea of having friendships with people you have never met in real life. Not every post is about *Lost*, but *Lost* is what everyone there has in common. No need to search for a topic of conversation, because there is no end of discussion topics in the land of *Lost*.

Very early in its existence, the atmosphere of The Fuselage was like a social club, which led to discussions of getting together in "real life" and having a fan party for *Lost*. Members of The Fuselage's predecessor, The Bronze: Beta, used to organize annual fan parties, and these became the basis for this fan party idea that was quickly becoming a hot topic of conversation in late 2004, mere months after the board went live. A handful of members from the Beta had put together what they called "PBPS" (Posting Board Parties) for the fans of *Buffy the Vampire Slayer* (and then *Angel*) who posted on the Beta. The PBPS were much

83

more laid-back than the "official" conventions typically associated with shows that have a cult following. They were held once a year in Los Angeles, with the only real structured part of the weekend being the charity VIP party that was usually held at the same hotel where everyone stayed. When talk about a *Lost* fan party became serious, the same event company that arranged the PBPS, EMA, took on this event as well, naming it "Destination: L.A." or "DLA" for short. DLA would be held in Los Angeles as well, with a block of rooms being held at the Hollywood and Highland Center at the Renaissance Hotel (the "Ren"), smack in the heart of Hollywood.

The main event would also be a charity VIP soiree, held on the Saturday evening of the weekend-long gathering in one of the ballrooms of the Ren. A silent auction, all the proceeds of which would be donated to J.J. Abrams' favorite charity, the Children's Defense Fund, would take place during the VIP party, where rare and much sought-after *Lost*-related goods (like signed scripts) would be up for auction. Following the successful tradition of the PBPS, the VIPS from the show would not be paid appearance fees to appear at the party, but rather were sent formal invitations asking them to come meet fans and help raise money for charity. Fan attendees were told in advance that no VIP attendance would be guaranteed, but some of the VIPS who were posting on The Fuselage did say they would be attending, which increased the buzz for the event.

The first DLA event was set for the second weekend of April 2005. Though The Fuselage was filled with party talk, most of the other *Lost* sites on the web were either clueless that the event was taking place or thought it was strictly for The Fuselage. DLA was never intended to be a party exclusively for members of The Fuselage, but that is what it was perceived to be. This perceived exclusivity prevented the event from generating a massive turnout, which was not necessarily a bad thing. It allowed it to be a much more intimate and laid-back affair. For the fan parties, the only "officially" scheduled events consisted of the Friday night "Pre-Party" (an icebreaker for the fans to finally meet each other face to face), the Saturday night charity VIP party, and the Sunday morning brunch. This spread-out schedule allowed those traveling long distances and those who had never been to Los Angeles before time to do some tourist things. Outings to Disneyland, the Magic Castle, the Jimmy Kimmel show and visits to the beach are some examples. A loose schedule also gives the various fanclubs that exist on the TB of The Fuselage a chance to schedule their own smaller meet-ups over the course of the weekend.

As DLA1 was approaching, two fanclubs decided to do more than just meet over the long weekend — they decided to compete. Hijinx was the leader of the Burky Babes, executive producer Bryan Burk's fan group (see "Breaking Down the Wall" on p. 73 for more details). She wanted the gathering to be more than just a bunch of fans meeting at a restaurant and watching each other eat. The gathering could be both interactive and relaxing, so bowling seemed like the perfect solution. Not being familiar with Los Angeles or the area of Hollywood that the hotel was located in, hijinx asked Javier Grillo-Marxuach the next time he popped up on the LB if there were any bowling alleys near the Ren. The request backfired a bit — Javi said that the Lucky Strike is right next to the Ren, then he asked, "Why? Do you think the javiminions should go bowling?" The "javiminions" is the name of Javi's fan group (of which hijinx is also a member). The initial plan had been to have a casual bowling event just for the Burky Babes, but Javi's comment led to an even better idea: turn it into a friendly bowling competition between the two clubs. Hijinx contacted Speaker, a good friend and the head of Javi's fanclub, to see if he would be interested in a collaboration. He thought it was a great idea as well. Bowlapalooza was born.

Bowlapalooza is now an annual competition between the Burky Babes and the javiminions, and has continued on even after Javi left the show to pursue other projects. The winning team gets bragging rights and a "classic" bowling trophy, which resides in the office of the winning team's VIP for a year. Burky and Javi have an odd sense of pride in displaying the 1982 bowling trophy that bears the name of hijinx's husband, who gave her permission to use it as the trophy for the event. The javiminions won the first Bowlapalooza competition, while the Babes took the trophy at the second (aka Bowlapalooza 2: Electric Boogaloo) and third (aka Bowlapalooza 3: Revenge of the Javi). Burky proudly displays the kitschy trophy in his office at Bad Robot, right next to his People's Choice and TCA awards.

The success of the Bowlapalooza event every year is mostly due to the presence of Javi. Even though he is no longer a writer for *Lost*, his influence on

William Mapother poses with goloptious at DLA2. She was the winning bidder on
Ethan Rom's lab coat worn in the episode "Maternity Leave."

the core development of the show and its characters has ensured that he will always be considered an important part of the *Lost* universe. His presence at the annual bowling event is as much for him as it is for his fans — and there is just nothing else like it. Each year when the dates for the fan party are announced, Javi is the first person hijinx calls to determine which night of the long weekend will work best for his schedule to hold Bowlapalooza. It is his opportunity to spend time with his fans in a more organic, one-on-one setting that extends far beyond what one would normally experience at a convention.

Which brings us to the heart of the difference between the annual *Lost* fan parties and the lone "Official *Lost* Convention" that was held in June of 2005: accessibility. At the official convention, put on by Creation

>: "Javi is tied up, Misery-style right now. I am forcing him to find a way to write the character of 'Steve' back into the show. This is why you haven't heard from him."
— Damon Lindelof, 2/18/05

>: "He is a stern taskmaster indeed — for those of you who do not know, Damon's weapon of choice is a giant whisk, and he wields it mightily!"
— Javier Grillo-Marxuach, 8/30/05

>: "Awwwww! Hijinx! One of my very favorite bunnies. It was wonderful meeting you, too. And thank you for the sweet words! I would have been happy to come home with you in your luggage. Just keep me dry and don't feed me after midnight and everything will be cool! And of course I will always come by to visit. I love to pet the bunnies."
— Andrea Gabriel (who plays Nadia, Sayid's love), 9/13/05

(All quotations from TheFuselage.com)

Entertainment, the fans had to pay to get their photos taken and to get an autograph from one of the actors from the show. Other people from the creative side of *Lost*, like writer and co-creator Damon Lindelof, executive producer Bryan Burk and the other members of the creative team present at the convention were not even included as an option for photo ops or autographs. The most direct interaction fans got was when they got up to ask a question at one of the panels. There was little to no personal communication at all.

William Mapother, who plays the recurring "Other" Ethan Rom on *Lost*, has attended two of the *Lost* fan parties and also participated in the Official

Lost Convention. At the convention, he was put up on a stage with Mira Furlan (Rousseau) and took questions from those fans who were able to get up to the microphone before time ran out. At the fan parties, he was able to mingle with the fans, who would patiently wait their turn in little unorganized clusters around him. No pressure. No standing in a long line, waiting to spend 30 seconds with him to snap a picture and get an autograph. There are no time limits at the fan parties, and all of the fans in attendance were respectful enough to not take too much of his time. Mapother attended the two DLA parties, but was unable to make the third fan party, called LOST Weekend and held in March 2007, because he was filming for another role. His absence at the event was felt by his fans, who all signed a posterboard that was eventually sent to him. Mapother admits to preferring the atmosphere of the fan parties over the convention. In his words, "The parties were smaller and allowed more interaction with fans." If you take a look through the pictures from DLA1 and DLA2, it is plainly evident that William was having a nice time with the fans.

The access to VIPs found on The Fuselage spilled over into these fan parties. Though the VIPs are offered security personnel, they are often not needed for anything other than keeping the crowds surrounding a VIP from getting too big and directing said VIPs to the bar and the bathrooms. The fans who frequent The Fuselage seem to appreciate this unprecedented access, both online and at the fan parties, and they work hard to make sure the VIPs are treated well — for fear of losing that special bond.

The first *Lost* fan party, DLA1 held in April 2005, was undoubtedly the most well attended, by both VIPs and fans. Though most of the main characters were unable to attend due to ABC adding episodes to the end of the season, two stars did manage to make it — Harold Perrineau (Michael) and Daniel Dae Kim (Jin), who were flown in to Los Angeles after they finished filming their scenes from the finale. To make up for the dearth of main actors, someone from inside *Lost* filmed a video that aired exclusively at the VIP party in which the cast members who couldn't make it taped messages for the partygoers. It was abundantly clear that the actors and those who worked on the show were very appreciative of the *Lost* fanbase. Even the actors who portrayed the backstory characters were eager to meet the fans as well. The names of John Terry (Dr. Christian Shephard), Zack Ward (Jack's best man in the wedding flashback), Neil Hopkins (Liam Pace) and Andrea Gabriel (Sayid's lost love, Nadia) may not be as recognizable to those outside the fandom, but to the fans attending DLA they are well known. The party organizers put out feel-

Daniel Dae Kim appears to be telling Carencey how relieved he is to be at Destination: L.A. 1 without Jin's handcuffs.

ers on The Fuselage, asking which secondary characters the fans would like to see invited. Now, many of those actors make an effort to come to the party every year — even if their character has been killed off. Daniel Roebuck played Dr. Arzt and has only appeared in a handful of episodes, plus one of the *Lost*: Missing Pieces "mobisodes," but he enjoys coming to the *Lost* fan parties (he's attended two so far) where he finally gets to interact with his fans face to face, something he hasn't always had a chance to do.

In an industry that has traditionally set up barriers and massive amounts of security to keep the stars separated from the fans, for their own "protection," the DLA and LOST Weekend parties are unprecedented celebrations without those restrictions. Of course, the smaller, more intimate nature of the fan parties definitely work in their favor. Organizers have put a cap on the number of attendees to make sure the event is kept conducive to the VIPs' freedom to mingle comfortably without hordes of fans surrounding them — though at this point no fans have been turned away. At the first DLA, Greg Grunberg (the pilot of Flight 815) showed up unexpectedly to the great delight of the fans. Though his role on *Lost* didn't survive past the pilot episode, he is well known for his other roles in *Heroes*, and on *Felicity* and *Alias*, which were both created by Greg's friend since childhood, J.J. Abrams. He arrived earlier in the evening and had a consistently large crowd around him for most of the event. The fans were respectful — never crowding, waiting patiently for their turns — and Greg was amenable to all of them. He posed for photos, signed autographs and even talked on cell phones to mothers and friends of those in attendance. He had no security people around him all evening, and never seemed to need any.

The only VIP who has actually needed security to help with the crowd attention was J.J. Abrams, who attended DLA1. His possible attendance was kept a secret. Only a handful of people knew, in case he had to cancel at the last minute. But when he was five minutes away, the word spread quickly throughout the attendees, and his arrival resulted in a juggernaut crowd outside the ballroom where the VIP party was being held. J.J. is viewed as geek royalty, and his presence was a very big treat for the fans. If the event had been a convention, however, the best a fan could have hoped for would be a good seat for a panel he was participating in (only obtained after waiting in line for hours), and a fevered dream of bumping into him in the hall, possibly managing to get a photo, an autograph and maybe a bit of conversation. But at DLA1, even with one or two security personnel, if you wanted a few moments with J.J., it wasn't that difficult to get. He was incredibly congenial — as likable in person, if not more so, than you could imagine.

Towards the end of the first VIP party, J.J. and Damon took the stage, along with all of those actors and producers in attendance, and they were given the chance to address the crowd. J.J. spoke first, mainly thanking the fans for their loyalty and support, and attributing the success of *Lost* to the fans: "The fact that it got on the air, and that you embraced it the way you did and allowed it to live — it is just an extraordinary gift to us . . . it wouldn't exist without you guys." Abrams then specifically mentioned how The Fuselage had contributed to making the show successful: "The dialogue of doing a series, especially for a show like *Lost*, is crucial. Because not only did you guys embrace it and let us keep doing the show, but it's more than that. It's the energy we get from you guys. It truly is the thing that allows us to keep going. Your enthusiasm is the thing that fuels us."

When Damon Lindelof took over the mic he echoed J.J.'s sentiments about the fans, especially the Fuselagers in attendance. He also talked about how, not long ago, he was just another fan like us. "A year ago, I was you guys. I was a fan of *Lost* and *Buffy* [*the Vampire Slayer*] and *Angel* . . . posting on these sites and sort of nitpicking episodes, picking favorite characters and coming to events like this. And now to be sort of up on this stage and still feeling like I'm a part of this community, but also feeding this community, is probably

The attendees of the first ever Bowlapalooza had a great time with the objects of their devotion — Javier Grillo-Marxuach and Bryan Burk (both lying down on the greasy bowling alley floor in the front of the group).

the most exciting thing that has ever happened to me on a professional level, let alone a personal one." Lindelof, Abrams and all of the other creators of the *Lost* universe who were at DLA1, and at the future parties, have embraced the opportunity to talk directly to the "superfans" of *Lost* while expressing a kinship with them via The Fuselage and the fan parties. There have been no spit-and-polish soliloquies directed to a faceless mass via the press or other media outlet. Overall, their speeches and one-on-one conversations have all come from the heart.

Though the subsequent fan parties, DLA2 that was held in May 2006 and LOST Weekend in March 2007, cannot boast the same level of VIP or fan attendance as DLA1, they have still managed to bring in some impressive support from *Lost* Labs. Bryan Burk has been to the fan parties every year they have been held, and he makes a huge effort to see the event supported internally. He also tries to get at least one or two of the big-name actors to attend, if at all possible. But for the Fuselagers, the attendance of many of the creative team members from *Lost* has been just as significant as the actor attendance, if not more so.

That speaks to the nature of this fandom — the genius of those behind the camera is just as recognized and fawned over as the amazing performances in front of it.

The fan parties have never been a huge success in terms of making money, and attendance has remained at a very modest level. It is surprising, considering the size of the *Lost* fandom and the lack of a second "official" *Lost* convention. For those who do attend, the experience typically surpasses their expectations. When asked why he attends every year, Bryan Burk responded, "The fans go — that's why I go. The fact that people take the time and money to travel great distances for no other reason than to celebrate our show is the most flattering thing in the world." The fans come from all over the U.S. — and a few come from other countries like Ireland, Germany and Wales. At any other convention, including the official one, VIPs such as Maggie Grace (Shannon) and Harold Perrineau would be hidden away until it was time for their panel. They might sit for a spell, sign autographs and allow pictures to be taken of them with a line of anonymous fans, but they'd never get the chance to exchange more than a few words or any length of time with these people who traveled from far and wide to attend.

The first two *Lost* fan parties were organized by "EMA" — Events by Maya and Allyson. Their involvement in the first party was due largely to Allyson's friendship with first season *Lost* writer and co-executive producer David Fury. When the time came to start planning DLA2, Fury was no longer with *Lost*, so EMA was not so sure they wanted to handle another party. But with support from the fans at The Fuselage, they decided to organize it. After many hurdles (including having to move the party to Pasadena due to a huge conference in L.A. taking up all of the hotels on the chosen weekend) DLA2 took place in May of 2006.

At the DLA2 VIP party, rumors spread that EMA was not interested in hosting any more *Lost* fan parties. This caused some anxiety for those fans in attendance who caught wind of it. A number of them approached hijinx, determining that her connections to Bad Robot and *Lost* Labs would make her the best candidate to take over the parties. Hijinx agreed to look into the possibility — and she got so far as to give the next party a new name, "LOST Weekend," and picking a weekend in mid-spring 2007. In the late fall of 2006, hijinx realized that she could not give the time and attention necessary to make LOST

Weekend a success, so she turned over the reins of the party arrangements to three other longtime fans of *Lost*, and fellow Fusers: halfrek, Carencey and OldManFan.

The *Lost* fan parties are unique, and the fans who attend come away with a different perspective of the people behind the show. The group of fans who attend every year, most of whom comprise the Usual Suspects referred to in The Fuselage chapter (p. 19), shared an unparalleled experience at DLA1. It has created a bond amongst people from a cornucopia of backgrounds — this same group comes back year after year. There was no fan party held in 2008, due to the WGA strike, but the organizers are already planning a LOST Weekend in 2009. If they manage to put together a party for 2010, as well, that event will undoubtedly be the ultimate celebration for the fans, the creators and the actors of *Lost*. It should be a fitting swan song.

Chapter 10

LIVING *LOST*

By DocArzt

I NEVER EXPECTED I'd make it to "The Island" in my lifetime. In this case, the island of Oahu, where *Lost* is filmed. Nonetheless, in late October, when the fall temperatures of my native Maine were beginning to dip to below 50 degrees, I found myself in the air heading towards the Pacific paradise. The reason I was there was that the producers of *Lost* had extended me an invite to visit the set (see page 139). Yet the set visit would be only one half of my adventure on "The Island." The other half rested in the hands of some industrious locals.

Oahu will always be an island of mystery for me in one regard. When we came in for a landing on the landmass that doubles as *Lost*'s mysterious island, the visibility was so poor in the air I could only see a thick mist. As we made our approach to the runway, the mist thinned and we were able to see perhaps a mile of the island on either side of the runway. My hope for an aerial view of the entire island was dashed.

When we got off the plane the heat was at first oppressive. A common phrase in the northeast of the mainland is: "It's not the heat, it's the humidity." This was certainly the case that day. My first comment about the oppressiveness

95

of the heat magically summoned a local security guard. Within minutes, he'd extracted information about our home base and names, given copious alohas to the kids, suggested beaches and given me a brief education on trade winds. "The winds have been slow for a couple of days," he says, "but they usually blow steadily, and when they do the atmosphere on the island can't be beat."

Within the next twelve hours or so, his prediction came true. How did this guy find the time to single us out from the bevy of newly minted tourists carousing through the airport?

I'd disregarded talk of the "aloha spirit" as really effective viral marketing up to this point, but it was true. It's not something you will find in every last niche and corner of the island, of course, but the reputation of the Hawaiian people for being laid-back, easygoing and good-natured is all too true.

Lana'i Lookout coast, one of *Lost*'s most dangerous shooting locales.

The assumption that everyone on the island watches *Lost* couldn't be further from the truth. After spending a couple of days there, you almost can't imagine people in this laid-back atmosphere getting into the tensions of the show's mystery, and the intense characters of *Lost*'s mysterious island. In fact, this subject comes up frequently during the tourist phase of our trip, mostly when people ask, "What brings you to Hawaii?" The majority of people we talk to are not fans, but almost all of them know one, or, through some social daisy-chain, know someone who has met someone associated with the show.

As we weave around the maze that is Waikiki's one-way infrastructure, we find ourselves spotting, as if by instinct, many of the urban locations for *Lost*. Even as we try desperately to find the right combination of turns to bring us to the parking garage for our hotel, we are bumping into the myriad worlds

Base camp at Camp Erdman. That is the food services trailer where it is rumored you can buy a crew shirt. I was not able to confirm. (Really . . . I wasn't.)

of *Lost*. A bridge here, a canal there, even storefronts seem familiar, and many are. In downtown Waikiki we find the stadium where Penny first tracked down Desmond before his fateful run with Jack. Los Angeles, Korea, New York, it's all here.

TOURMASTER OF "THE ISLAND"

All of the fans I have talked to who have visited the island of Oahu describe having their "moment," a sort of flash of intuition where you look around you and realize you are on "The Island." For me, the moment was when Ed Kos of Hummer Tours Hawaii drove me to the heart of the Kualoa Ranch pastures. When you stand on the open plain to which Sayid, Shannon, Sawyer, Kate and Boone hiked in an attempt to contact any rescuers with the transponder, when you stop and look around at the eroded foothills that flank the valley, suddenly, you are immersed in the world of *Lost*. For a moment I felt a bit like my son,

Ed Kos of Hummer Tours Hawaii.

who was not buying the idea that any of the show was real. To witness the landscape in three dimensions was surreal.

For Ed Kos, not so much. In contrast to the great sense of mystery that standing in the valley evokes for dyed-in-the-wool *Lost* fans, Kos has an understanding of the history of the area, and he can go into incredible detail. The former marine, now a tour guide, is an island historian first, and a *Lost* historian second. As we marvel at standing in the world of *Lost*, Kos is picking out minute flora details, explaining how they came to be on the island and recounting the rich history of the

>: "Oh my god! Is that DOM!… sorry, false alarm. This was just a test of the emergency Dom system. Had Dom really shown up on the fuselage, you would have received special Dom instructions. This concludes the test of the emergency Dom system."
— Javier Grillo-Marxuach, 7/30/05

>: "Anyone: What the H does lol mean?"
— Terry O'Quinn, 8/13/05

>: "Okay, Carencey. If you insist on shouting at me… Locke slipped in the bathtub. Happy now? Just kidding."
— Damon Lindelof, 9/15/05

settlement and agriculture of the island. Suddenly I feel a bit like an invader, a castaway inadvertently dropped onto a natural wonder that should be insulated from mankind.

Kos has done general "movie" tours for years, taking tourists to the various locations used in such films as *Mighty Joe Young*, *Pearl Harbor*, *Jurassic Park* and television shows like *Magnum PI*. Still, Kos tells me his transition to offering a *Lost*-only tour was a slow one. More of a demand-meets-supply kind of thing. Kos's canvas is the island of Oahu itself. You can hear it in his voice when he discusses the history of the island. Kos is no opportunist, and the secrets of *Lost* are safe with him. Respecting the privacy of the crew is tantamount, though it often results in a battle of wills with his clients. If you're looking to crash a *Lost* shooting, don't expect Kos to deliver you.

As Kos takes me from location to location I learn that his business was not initially very focused on *Lost*. During the average day of taking tourists around the island's most stunning natural locations and historic buildings, the tour guide had organically run into the *Lost* crew's numerous location shoots.

Though he was not really a fan of the show, Kos began putting time into learning some of the show's iconic scenes so he could attempt to match them up as he took tourists around. A fair number of his finds came from *Lost* fans themselves who had pointed out surprisingly minute landmarks that gave away certain scenes or locations. The stump that Goodwin and Ana Lucia sat on, the Banyan tree from the pilot. A *Lost* fan's love for minutiae is matched only by Kos's keen memory of the island's geography. Fans come wanting the most obscure of *Lost*'s locations revealed, and Kos delivers.

RISKING YOUR LIFE FOR GOOD TV

For visitors to the island of Oahu looking to make their own way around,

This is one side of the rope bridge that Charlie and Hurley crossed in "Numbers."

LostVirtualtours.com (LVT) has you covered. Run by a Hawaiian fan of *Lost*, the site has the distinction of being steeped in the lore and fervent interest of the show. Completeness and accuracy is an imperative here, and it reaches a level only a *Lost* fan could understand. My day out with one of the proprietors of the site is a testament to their never-say-die mission to make the site's location charts, maps and photos the most complete in the world. Literally.

One of the locations we visit is the Lana'i Lookout coast. This patch of coastline first appeared in "The Other 48 Days" as the bizarre and forbidding eroded rock over which Ana Lucia led the remaining tailsection survivors, along with Michael, Sawyer and Jin, in their trek to get to the fuselage beach. Later, this almost alien coastline would appear in the season 2 finale as the area where Desmond accidentally kills hatchmate Kelvin.

The Kos tour had shown me how the crew had been willing to pack in a pretty good hike to get to "just the right" location, but the visit with the LVT webmaster to the Lana'i Lookout was testament to how the cast and crew were willing to risk it all.

Greeting you at the edge of the steep incline leading down to where those shots were filmed is a sign that clearly reads "Hazardous Conditions: Do Not Go Beyond This Point." And for good reason. The walk down to the shooting arena is a matter of picking the right plateau to jump to. The surface is volcanic rock, and the perpetual erosion creates an ever-present dust that is far more slippery than it looks. Looking closely at the dust reveals hundreds of tiny, perfect spheres. Walking along the ledge is like walking on a sea of microscopic marbles.

As we get closer to the coast, my friend from LVT tells me to pay careful attention to any signs of wet rock. Sudden surges can reach surprisingly far inland and with incredible force, enough to snatch you off your feet and into the roiling waves below. Once in the water, the waves would throw your body like a rag doll against the steep cliff below. This isn't an exaggeration, it has happened — more often than not to tourists, like us, who ignored the copious warnings above.

In fact, the history of the area is full of terrifying tales of death. Even hardcore divers are reluctant to test the waters. A relative of a victim who was swept off the coast recounted to *Shorediving* magazine that "I jumped in after her and I grabbed her. We held each other, but the water just kept throwing us against the rocks. I got to her but the undertow and waves were so strong. They'd yank us to the bottom and we'd swim to the top. I remember going down real deep, then being all alone. I remember coming up and not being able to see her anymore. Then three guys woke me up on the rocks."

The threat to the *Lost* crew and cast is just as real. The location is difficult to navigate, even with nothing more to manage than a handheld camera. It is difficult to imagine being loaded down with a steadicam rig, or being asked to simply ignore the hazards long enough to look like you are intent on nothing but reaching your dramatized goal.

Even on Ed Kos's more conservative tour, the rigors of the natural locations have a chilling testament. One remote location Kos led me to, the clearing that doubled as the vacuum tube dump for the Pearl station, had me nearly breathless by the time we reached it. Kos said that he had seen tourists unprepared for the hike drop from heatstroke, or diabetic shock. Hydration, Kos told me, was the number one issue for visitors not used to the climate. Tourists would tend to lug around sodas or juice and sweat their supply of water away, inviting exhaustion and sickness. For the unacclimated, like myself, the results could be deadly.

The earlier forays into the *Lost* visit had me increasingly concerned about what kind of rigors the real crew might be preparing to put me through. Thankfully, after coming face to face with the island's dangers, and earning a new respect for *Lost*'s dedication to getting just the right shot, ABC contacted me and told me that my destination would be Camp Erdman — aka New Otherton. My only endurance test would be navigating the Hawaiian infrastructure and a short ride in a production shuttle. No cliff walls to scale, rigorous hikes to challenge my middle-aged deconditioning or horror stories of unprepared tourists falling face first into the rich Hawaiian soil. The only danger remaining in my journey to *Lost*'s island was the anxiety of facing the flesh-and-blood personages of the *Lost* cast and crew. That, as they say, is another story.

Chapter 11

CASTING: TALES
OF LOVE AND HATE

LOST FANS ARE, to be sure, increasingly possessive of the show as it goes
along, particularly when it comes to the characters. This is not to say that they
have a latent bad attitude, but this sense of "owning" the show and its character
narrative in particular has lead to a sort of realization amongst the fanbase that
when they are united on whether an actor works or doesn't work in a particular
role, they can seemingly anticipate the fate of those characters on the show.

Many actors have clamored for a chance to be on *Lost*. Before there was
even a script for the show, the mere idea that J.J. Abrams was casting this
potentially epic drama perked up many a struggling actor's ears — and at least
peaked the curiosity of those who have been in the biz for a while. The show
has been heralded from the beginning as a stage where breakthrough performances can take place. In reality, much of the cast are debatably veterans of one
form or another, while others were just waiting for their big break. Matthew
Fox had 142 episodes of *Party of Five* under his belt, but Josh Holloway had a
string of roles like "good-looking guy" and "Lana's Toyboy" on his resume and
he was briefly considering a career in real estate before *Lost* came along.

Lost has become a point of historic character turns for practically every

Maggie Grace (Shannon), Sam Anderson (Bernard) and Daniel Roebuck (Dr. Arzt)
have all found success on the island of *Lost* fans.

actor involved from the beginning, regardless of his or her background. Jorge Garcia will have as hard a time disassociating himself with Hurley as Terry O'Quinn will have shaking the John Locke moniker. They have each become their own personal Gilgamesh in the most epic of modern mythologies, completely inseparable from *Lost*'s place in history. But not every actor to shuffle along the sands of Oahu to the show's surrealistic groove has fared so well.

Some fans are quick to dismiss the way the character narrative seems to flow with the voicing of approval and displeasure, but as time has gone on there are some indications that the will of the fanbase has been acknowledged by the "powers that be." Javier Grillo-Marxuach, supervising producer and writer for *Lost* during the first two seasons, acknowledges that, "To some degree, if the fans clamor for a certain character or things like that . . . fans can be very influential." But, he also cautions that in the end, "Most show creators are very autocratic and they will do what they will do."

William Mapother did not have to audition for his role as Ethan Rom. J.J. Abrams cast him based on Mapother's performance as Richard Strout in the movie *In the Bedroom*, and he was initially only signed on for two episodes. But his turn as the first "Other" the Losties — and the audience — encounter on the island made such an impression on the producers and the viewers that Ethan has shown up in more episodes post-mortem than he did alive. The organic nature of the *Lost* Writers' Room allowed them to continue to find uses

Jorge Garcia will long be remembered for his portrayal of Hurley on *Lost*.
One wonders if he'll ever tire of hearing and saying the word "dude."

for a character who had intrigued the fans and used him to introduce the mysterious Others.

An even better example of a secondary character becoming more popular than originally anticipated is Michael Emerson. Emerson was originally contracted to play the mysterious Henry Gale for only three episodes. The producers were so enthralled with his performance that they continued renewing his contract. The decision to continue on with Emerson in the role of Gale, and later as the leader of the Others, preceded the public's first glance at the actor's chilling delivery. Later it would be revealed that although the character of Ben Linus had already been conceived at this point, the idea that it was Linus posing as Henry Gale had not. Again the writers' flexibility allowed them to merge what was originally conceived as two separate characters into a single, more dynamic character, while keeping true to the "big picture."

A murkier example can be found in Michelle Rodriguez's Ana Lucia Cortez. Ana Lucia was introduced in the season 1 finale as a tentative love interest for Jack; someone he had met at the airport and had shared a definable "moment" with. By the time the callous Sawyer-beater made her way from the tail section crash site to the fuselage camp in season 2, fans were beginning to grumble about Rodriguez's patented "tough chick" cliché. Cliché was a word not often used in relation to *Lost*, and the insertion of what was considered a carbon copy of Rodriguez's earlier character types who was slapping around fan favorites didn't sit well with the show's more protective fans.

Ana Lucia had her supporters, but all attempts to redeem the character on the show seemed to fall flat. Even when it was eventually revealed that Ana Lucia had lost a baby due to the reckless acts of a violent criminal, fans were quick to point out that she too was a cold-blooded murderer because she eventually got revenge by pumping the creep full of lead in a dark alley. After the episode "Collision" aired, Damon Lindelof came onto The Fuselage to address the fan reactions, immediately acknowledging that the bulk of the comments were negative ones about Ana Lucia. His response to the negativity was this: "Well, what can we say? Some characters you sympathize with, others you don't. Just remember . . . it's a long (and winding) road." One fan questioned whether or not Lindelof and the other members of the creative team at least "read the road signs," to which Damon replied: "We totally read the signs. And we follow our guts. Controversy is a good thing. Love her, hate her . . . Ana Lucia is there just like everyone else . . . [f]or a reason." Ana Lucia just couldn't get a break, not even from her creators.

Just prior to Ana Lucia's eventual exit from the show, Michelle Rodriguez and costar Cynthia Watros (Libby) were both stopped, individually, for operating under the influence (OUI) in Hawaii. Rumors swirled that the actresses would be cut from the show due to the scandal, so when they were both gunned down by Michael in the episode "Two for the Road," the audience reaction partly dulled the writers' attempt to craft a truly horrifying scene. At least one of the characters, by some estimation, "got what she deserved," while the other was being booted from the show for behaving badly.

The producers, of course, denied everything, and when Libby was brought back to the show it was to tremendous enthusiasm from the fans. Libby, as it turns out, is a more integral part of the story than we might have imagined.

To the credit of the show's creators, the number of disliked characters who are killed off is roughly equal to the number of characters who prove to be fan favorites. Boone and Shannon had their detractors, for sure, but their deaths were hardly celebrated the way Ana Lucia's was. The days of denying that the audience was signing death warrants would soon come to an end in season 3, with the introduction of Nikki and Paulo.

Season 3 brought an interesting notion to the *Lost* Writers' Room: what if some of the background characters — from the mostly nameless mass seen wandering about in the background at the beach — suddenly stepped forward and became part of the ensemble? The idea was not without precedent. They had introduced the character of Dr. Leslie Arzt in this way, and though his character was short-lived, the fans seemed to accept him. Should we pretend that those blurry forms busying themselves just outside the range of the camera's focus are unaware of the Dharma Initiative, or don't dodge the occasional polar bear? As it turns out, the answer is, for the most part . . . yes.

When Nikki and Paulo first appeared (Nikki in episode 3.03, "Further Instructions," and Paulo in episode 3.04, "Every Man for Himself"), the col-

(All quotations from TheFuselage.com)

>: "Man, you guys are BRUTAL on the Ana Lucia tip… Well, what can we say? Some characters you sympathize with, others you don't. Just remember… it's a long (and winding) road. I still love you all."
— Damon Lindelof, 11/24/05

"Jinx, We totally read the signs. And we follow our guts. Controversy is a good thing. Love her, hate her . . . Ana Lucia is there just like everyone else… For a reason."
— Damon Lindelof, 11/24/05

"Don't get me started on the Scott/Steve issue. Seriously."
— Damon Lindelof, 2/18/05

lective fandom groaned. For once, the *Lost* fans were united in their displeasure. The casting practically screamed "Note from Studio: Cast a couple of hot young actors to absorb the Boone/Shannon demographic." So they were quickly given less-than-flattering nicknames, such as Castaway Barbie and Ken. The ludicrousness of the stunt was even more pronounced for those who remembered Damon and Carlton repeatedly stating that part of the problem with the characters of Boone and Shannon was that they were so young they did not have enough life experience for more than a few flashbacks. Why, then, cast two equally young actors for roles that were tertiary at best?

Thankfully, the audience was spared from too much Nikki and Paulo. As annoying as they were as living, breathing characters, their "deaths" were gruesomely entertaining. The writers proved that they had a sense of humor about the whole thing, though that humor is decidedly twisted, to say the least. The episode "Exposé" gave *Lost* fans Billy Dee Williams, more Shannon/Boone/Ethan/Dr. Arzt, the "meatsocks" perspective from the pilot episode and a Twilight Zone–esque ending that will creep out fans for years to come. The characters themselves may be easily forgotten, but their demise will be hard to forget.

"Exposé" reflected the discomfort of the creators in the subtext of the episode's overarching plot. Nikki and Paulo were two characters who were never really given a chance by the audience, so how symbolically fitting is it that the duo were buried alive onscreen, paralyzed by the bite of Dr. Arzt's Medusa spider and by the apathy and disdain of an equally venomous audience?

The elimination of Nikki and Paulo is a rare instance of the showrunners admitting that fan reaction guided the writers' hands. It is dangerous for any show to openly admit that the fans have that much say, but as much as the writers want and hope everything will go according to plan, it is an impossible goal to achieve. The good news for the fans is that *Lost*'s showrunners and the creative team have gone to great lengths to not only entertain the audience but to actively listen to them, as well. The result is that subsequent cast additions, whether long-term or short-term, have been handled better by the writers, and thus these new characters are more accepted by the fans in general.

No one wants the story well to run dry or go stale; the best way to prevent that from happening is to bring in new characters to "shake things up." That is the premise behind the other popular television shows currently on the air — *CSI*, *Law & Order* and *Grey's Anatomy* have new victims/criminals/patients each week. Their main characters are confronted with new characters and situations every episode. But that is difficult to pull off when all of your main characters are stranded on a mysterious island. Flashbacks and flash-forwards have allowed the *Lost* fans to encounter new and intriguing circumstances and people, but there has to be something fresh for the on-island stories as well, otherwise we would definitely be at the point where coconut bowling was a common occurrence. Thankfully, the creative team at *Lost* has used its close proximity to its fanbase to learn from their mistakes, as well as to take advantage when a character, like Henry Gale, does strike a chord, even if it was not expected.

Chapter 12

SHIPPER WARS

Bangel. Spuffy. Cordangel.
S/V. Sarkney. Sweiss.
Literati. Rogan. Narco. PDLD. JavaJunkie.
MerDer. Gizzie.

IF YOU HAVE NEVER participated on an online fan forum for a television drama series, then the terms above probably mean nothing to you. The list above is composed of what are known as "shipper" names for fans of various television shows' most popular relationships. If you were a fan of the Jess/Rory relationship on *Gilmore Girls*, then you "ship" Literati (called that because of the two characters' love of books and because they were constantly being shown reading on screen). Another way to put it is, you are a Literati shipper. If you believe that Spike and Buffy were soulmates on *Buffy the Vampire Slayer*, then you are a Spuffy. Long after a show ends, the ships live on through fanfiction and fanart on various online sites and journals. Shippers can be hugely supportive of the show their favorite ship is on, or they can rip the show to shreds because they don't like how their favorite ship is being handled. There is nothing quite as brutal in the land of online forums as a shipper group scorned — and they have *long* memories.

The *Lost* fandom has many ships, which isn't surprising considering the number of main characters. But there is no doubt about which shipper groups are the largest and most prevalent on the boards: the Jaters and the Skaters. "Jaters" ship the Jack and Kate relationship, while "Skaters" ship Kate with Sawyer. The Jaters and Skaters started out like any other shipper groups, but as the seasons have progressed, so has the intensity level of the group members. In fact, things became so heated between the groups during season 3 that the moderators ("Mods") at The Fuselage were forced to take an extreme measure to keep the peace. They decided to lock the Jater and Skater discussion threads; you would be required to get Mod approval before you could join one of the groups. What happened that led to this forced separation? To attempt to understand that, first you have to know more about shippers in general.

If there has never been a psychological examination of shipperdom, then there should be one. The way that a certain television viewer's perception of a scene is tainted by the amount of devotion they feel for their favored ship is truly fascinating. For example, in *Lost* episode 3.16, "One of Us," Jack, Kate and Sayid return to the beach camp with Juliet in tow. For Skaters, the look on Sawyer's face when he sees Kate again and their prolonged hug when they reunite was clear evidence that those two characters wanted to be together. For Jaters, the vulnerability on Sawyer's face was evidence of his weakness as a man, which Kate merely felt sorry for and gave him a pity hug. If your shipper preference tends to lean outside of the canonical box, then the fact that Kate hugged Hurley first and with obvious emotion made the Haters (a Hurley-Kate shipper group) wild with happiness. The Jawyers (Jack-Sawyer slash shippers) were squealing with glee that Sawyer was not satisfied with a mere handshake from Jack, so he pulled him into an electrifying hug that was ripe with unspoken emotion. It's all in the psychology of perception.

A *Lost* writer does not sit at his or her computer and say, "Now how am I going to please/tick off the Jaters in this episode?" For the writer, it is the character development and plot that are of primary concern. Having Kate and

Sawyer get carnal in the bear cage was more about its effect on Jack, and Ben's plans for Jack, than it was an affirmation for the Skaters. Try telling that to a Skater, though.

Damon Lindelof and Carlton Cuse have had the luxury of addressing the shipper questions on their podcasts with lightness, humor and their ever-present snark. They have accused each other of being either a Jater or a Skater, and on one occasion even stated that one of them is a Jater and the other one a Skater, but that they would not reveal who was which. Whether they are aware of the impact that their every comment or subtle innuendo about these relationships has on the shipper threads of the *Lost* forums is unclear. It is best to hope that they are blissfully unaware — otherwise something like their decision to tell the fans that the "triangle" (Jack/Kate/Sawyer) would be "resolved" in season 3 could be seen as being downright cruel to the Mods on those forums who have had to deal with the cleanup ever since.

At the San Diego Comic Con held in late July 2006, a fan asked the *Lost* panel, "When the heck is Kate going to get with somebody?" Damon's response was this: ". . . within the first six episodes [referring to season 3] . . . she'll be officially making her selection." If you happened to be standing close to the Internet at the time that piece of information hit the airwaves, you may have heard a loud "BOOM" as the Jater and Skater shippers imploded like the hatch. It's one thing to see a television scene that can be deciphered in a variety of ways, depending on the viewer's own personal shipper leanings. But to have the *showrunner* make a statement like that was the equivalent of pulling the pin on a grenade, throwing it into the shipper threads, then slamming the door just as it all blows up. When the infamous Kate and Sawyer "sex in a bear cage" episode aired, it seemed that the choice had been made. The Skaters acted like they had just won the Super Bowl or the World Cup. They were doing their version of celebrating in the end zone. And hey, what's celebrating without a little showboating? In this case, it was a litany of "I told you so" posts. Well, the Jaters weren't about to bow out gracefully, so they came up with plenty of rebuttals and dug into every interview and podcast they could find, pulling out evidence that they believed proved that Kate might be with Sawyer now, but that Jack is her OTP (One True Pair) and in the end, Jack is who she'll be with. The shipper wars turned very ugly, very quickly.

Adding to the drama was the growing number of Jacket (Jack/Juliet) shippers. Since Juliet did not arrive on the show until season 3, the Jacket group was a smaller, quieter bunch at first. But the apparent "choice" made by Kate when she slept with Sawyer in episode 3.06 seemed to indicate to the Jacket shippers that they were right, along with the Skaters. A few episodes later, Jack and Juliet kiss, putting another feather in the Jacket cap. Though the animosity between the Jackets and Jaters was not quite at the level of the Jater/Skater war, things still got steadily uglier between those two groups as well.

So how does a shipper war get "ugly"? After all, it's just the Internet bulletin boards for *Lost* — the worst anyone can do is post mean or taunting messages in each other's threads, right? If it were only that simple. The posts were bad enough, but add to that some Skater/Jater/Jacket members who are skilled at fanart (i.e., icons, avatars, manips, videos, wallpapers, banners, lolcats) — the war escalated and got really personal, really fast. If you have spent any time around the *Lost* fans online, you should be aware of how intelligent most of them are, and they have an amazing capacity for sarcasm, both subtle and not so subtle. Slamming opposing shipper groups via graphics became common-place; so much so that the Mods at The Fuselage had to start issuing warnings and infraction points for avatars that could be considered to be "baiting" specific shipper groups.

When the shipper wars blew up on The Fuselage, the impact may not have been felt by the entire board, but it was definitely felt by the Mods. It is impossible to commiserate with the Mods at The Fuselage unless you are one of them. It is a truly thankless job, and it can suck the joy right out of you if you let it. The wars pushed the Mods to their absolute limits, with a seemingly never-ending string of reported posts. The various shipper groups were spying on the competing shipper threads, then reporting back in their own thread; then the other group would find out and they would do the same thing. It was a continuous vicious cycle with no real end in sight. On top of all that, the shippers began accusing certain Mods of favoritism. Every warning, every infraction was picked apart to identify its level of harshness. Tallies were kept and compared. It was impossible to make everyone happy. It wasn't just Skater vs. Jater or Jater vs. Jacket anymore; it was Skaters vs. *everyone*, Jaters vs. *everyone*, etc. The notion that a Mod could be "neutral" was a foreign concept to most of the shippers — even though the ability to handle a situation without bias is one of the main traits you need to be selected as a Mod in the first place.

The Mods had to come up with a way to try and corral the shipper groups and separate them or else the infraction points would continue to rise and more people would be banned, which nobody really wanted. The solution the Mods devised was to make each of the most volatile shipper threads — the Jaters, the Skaters and the Jackets — private. To view and post in one of these three threads, you had to declare your allegiance and request admittance. The Mods look at each request, then either allow or deny it. Again, if you have not spent much time around a forum with shipper threads, and maybe even if you have, this solution may seem a little extreme. And it was an extreme measure to take, but it was necessary, for the health of these shipper groups and the sanity of the Mods.

>: "At this stage if Jack and Kate were to get together, good narrative story structure would insist that they may be split apart and never get back together again. The same goes for Kate and Sawyer… I think Damon definitely has an idea of what he wants to happen and would stay true to his original vision."
— Gregg Nations, 5/27/06

>: "It would be nice if Kate chose an equilateral triangle but she may go for an isosceles, perhaps even an obtuse isosceles (which may make it more scalene but who's counting?). So will the Euclidians out there be upset? What about the Pythagoreans? Hopefully they won't stop watching the show (though who can tell about the Cervanennes). I think all sides will be able to coexist. It's going to be exciting to see."
— Gregg Nations, 9/7/06

>: "Kate is probably going to have to fight Sawyer for Hurley's heart. That hug that Hurley gave Sawyer in 'Tricia Tanaka is Dead' made Sawyer forget all about his stash and he actually helped Hurley with the van after that. Now tell me that isn't love. So should it be Huryer or HurSaw? Sawyley? Whatever it is, it's probably the love that dare not speak its name."
— Gregg Nations, 5/9/07

As season 4 arrived, it seemed that the choices had been made — Kate and Sawyer "hooked up" numerous times in season 3, while Jack and Juliet shared a kiss or two. The shippers were chomping at the bit for new scenes to pick apart and use as further proof of the inevitability of their OTP. Where Kate's choice of Sawyer in season 3 seemed definitive — putting to rest the triangle of Jack, Kate and Sawyer — season 4 made that choice seem murkier, and more tentative. In Kate's future flash in episode 4.04, "Eggtown," Jack tells her that he lied on the stand when he said he didn't love her anymore. On the island story, Kate joined Jack's team that wanted to be rescued, while Sawyer chose to stay on the island with Team Locke. Kate was not happy about Sawyer's choice.

The love story of Bernard (played by Sam Anderson) and Rose (L. Scott Caldwell) is one of the more seaworthy ships of *Lost*.

Then came the episode "Something Nice Back Home" and once again the shipper wars blew up. In that episode's flash-forward, we learned that not only did Jack and Kate leave the island (sans Sawyer and Juliet, who were not part of the Oceanic 6), they shacked up together with baby Aaron and played house for some undetermined period of time. Back on the island, Juliet tells Kate that Jack kissed her, but believed it was only because he couldn't kiss someone else, the implication being that he wanted to kiss Kate. Just when the Jaters were on the verge of declaring victory, Kate admits to Jack in the flash-forward that she was secretly handling something for Sawyer. Jack flips out and reminds Kate that he was the one who "saved" her.

And just to make sure that the shippers are in complete disarray, the season 4 finale revealed that Sawyer was with those who eventually got rescued,

Taking a breather from the Shipper questions that flood his forum at The Fuselage, Gregg Nations gets ready to bowl for the Burky Babes at Bowlapalooza 3.

117

but sacrificed his chance by jumping out of the helicopter to guarantee that Kate (and the others on the helicopter) would make it. We see him whisper in her ear (what we assume to be her secret task), then he plants a lingering kiss on her (right in front of Jack) and jumps out into the ocean. Now that we know that at least three years pass before the Oceanic 6 make it back to the island, and it is implied that Juliet and Sawyer may believe that Jack, Kate and the rest of the helicopter occupants perished when the freighter blew up, there could be another ship forming from that infamous Love Square before it is all said and done.

The fact is, we won't know who "wins" in the shipper wars until the series is over. It would be a shame to be a fan so invested in your chosen shipper group that you come away from the end of *Lost* disappointed just because Kate did not end up with whomever it is you felt she should have ended up with.

Gregg Nations, script coordinator for *Lost*, has taken the brunt of the questions over the past couple of seasons from the various shipper groups who frequent The Fuselage. When asked whether or not the writers "take sides" in the shipper debate in the writers' room, this was his response:

> Honestly, I don't think the writers take either side of the shipper fans into consideration when they're thinking of Kate and her feelings towards Sawyer and Jack. I think that if they wrote the characters based on the risk of losing fans, the end result would be a mess. You have to create a character and let that character breathe and grow and make mistakes and feel like a real person. So when it comes to Kate's romantic feelings, I think they are more concerned with where Kate is as a character and where they want to take her.

Whether or not you can see aligning yourself with a particular relationship on your favorite television show, you can't help but appreciate the passion these *Lost* shippers have. The writers cannot just dismiss them (especially since they are responsible for creating the relationships that these fans have chosen to "ship") or their value to the show — that level of passion typically extends to watching the show every week, buying merchandise and telling people about the show. But hinging your like or dislike of a show on your shipper preference is a hopeless cause, especially if one character is considered central to the show.

As many television writers will tell you, a happy couple is a boring couple. This is especially true in dramatic television. Whereas with sitcoms it is possible to keep a couple together and make everything a punch line, there is no such luxury in primetime dramas. Call it the "Moonlighting" or "Sam and Diane" enigma. Either way, television history is rife with shows whose audiences lost interest once the favored ship finally set sail together.

The *Lost* creative team deserves at least some kudos for managing to present us with two married couples — Jin and Sun, and Rose and Bernard — who have both maintained interesting and believable story lines. It helps that Rose and Bernard are supporting cast, and so far have only had one flashback episode, plus a handful of "B" and "C" stories sprinkled over the seasons. But Jin and Sun are in the main cast of characters, and yet they have consistently been given story arcs that are not boring or soap operatic in nature — although, the brief "Who's the daddy?" responsible for Sun's pregnancy arc teetered very close to the latter. In the writers' favor, the Jin/Sun relationship is not one that started and had to be cultivated within the timeline of the show. Theirs was a relationship on the rocks that has gone through some very realistic ups and downs through the seasons of *Lost*. It's interesting to note that just when it appeared that everything was on track for Jin and Sun to get their "happily ever after" Disney ending (the baby is Jin's, they are getting rescued, Sun stopped lying about knowing English and stands up to Jin more, Jin isn't the domineering prick he was in season 1) we get the season 4 episode "Ji Yeon," and everything has been flipped upside down. Sun safely gives birth to their daughter back in Korea, but instead of Jin rushing to her side during the flash-forward . . . Sun visits his grave with Hurley. It was a brilliant twist to their love story, because the audience doesn't know if Jin is actually dead or possibly being held on the island as some sort of "insurance policy" to guarantee Sun's silence about what really happened to Oceanic Flight 815. The season 4 finale gave us one side of the story: Sun does believe that Jin is dead. She saw the freighter that he was on blow up as the helicopter that "rescued" the Oceanic 6 (plus Desmond and Frank) pulled away from the fiery explosion. Whether or not Jin is actually dead is still not certain in the minds of the audience, however — we saw him make it to the deck of the freighter, and there was a chance that he jumped overboard and survived the blast. Regardless, every scene between Jin and Sun from then on, until we learn the truth about Jin's fate, was tainted with the emotion of knowing that they will not be getting their happily ever after. Or so it seems.

What has worked so elegantly for the Jin/Sun (and Rose/Bernard) relationship is not possible to fully tap into for the newer relationships that have been developing since the plane crashed on the island. The Sawyer/Kate/Jack/Juliet "Love Square" (so named by Gregg Nations) will probably never be truly resolved until the end of the show, or the death of one or more of the involved parties. Towards the end of season 4, Damon had this to say about the fate of the Love Square:

> The people who are passionate about Jacket are very passionate, but ultimately the triangle is a product of Kate and will she end up with Jack or Sawyer. It's not like Carlton and I are both rooting for Jack on any given day. We feel like Kate's character is bound to explore relationships with both those guys and that both those guys are going to be responsive to her various advances. We know who she ends up with ultimately, but we think the trail leading there is obviously going to include a little bit of ping-ponging.

The other ships that were flirting with happiness to some degree — mainly Charlie/Claire and Hurley/Libby — have already been vanquished by the deaths of Charlie and Libby respectively. And though there is no guarantee that any shipper group will be 100 percent satisfied once the series finale rolls across our screens in the spring of 2010, there is no denying that the journey for the characters will be the furthest thing from "boring" one could possibly imagine. This is *Lost*, after all.

Chapter 13

DON'T TELL US
WHAT YOU CAN'T DO!

ONE OF THE MOST AMAZING aspects of the *Lost* phenomenon has been the creators' responsiveness to fans. No doubt the need to have a finger on the pulse of the audience was partially the impetus of The Fuselage; there is no better way to get a feel for how the audience is responding than to commingle with them. But was this rare level of access meant to allow the fans' reactions to have such a global impact behind the scenes? While there has never been admission to tweaking the overall story line to meet the taste of the Internet base, the creators have admitted that character deaths, the end of repeats, time slots and even the end of the show have all been influenced, in part, by dominant trends in fan opinion.

The sheer mass of the *Lost* fan community creates a voice that is difficult to ignore. Political elections are often swayed by the results of polls that sample fewer than 2000 people; collectively, the *Lost* Internet scene encompasses millions of fans worldwide, and frequently, opinion-based polls on popular news sites and forums can receive in excess of 10,000 votes. It's this kind of accretion of sentiment that has fueled a sense of obligation to respond to fans from *Lost*'s upper echelon.

Damon Lindelof said in an interview conducted in March 2008, "We like the idea of being answerable to the show, that is to say if we do something the fans don't like we can come forward and apologize for it and explain what the thought process was for executing that story line. Or, vice versa, if we do something people really like we get to sort of pull that forward and explain, for instance, that we weren't able to do the flash-forward part of the story until they promised us an end to the show, and this is how we were able to end the show, and this is why we are doing three more seasons, and so on. The fans are owed those explanations,"

Lindelof has done exactly that numerous times, though not usually via regular media outlets, instead choosing to bring those explanations directly to the fans by posting on The Fuselage. Choosing to posit this information on a fan board is not necessarily an attempt to circumvent the usual critics and entertainment media, it is Damon bringing the information personally to those who he feels deserve the truth most — the *Lost* fans. His affinity with The Fuselage and the *Lost* fans who post there has been mentioned numerous times in this book, and even though the Lagers tend to be more positive about the show and its creators than other *Lost* sites are, there are detractors and unhappy fans who post there as well.

Damon has been known to post to the naysayers directly, but in the end, he is adamant that *Lost* is not a show for everybody — there are those who "get it" and those who don't. The apologies and explanations given to the mass media by Lindelof and Carlton Cuse are much more politically correct when compared to the way Damon addresses issues on The Fuselage. Whether or not ABC is aware of his candidness on the Fuse, without the spit and polish of their public relations department, is unknown; but the benefit to the fans, and, in turn, to the creators, is incomparable. His decision to use The Fuselage has given him and the show a firm and faithful fanbase at that site, where he is accepted and embraced as a member of the community.

The power has become sort of an Ouroboros device for the more vocal fan set; a snake swallowing its own tail, a cycle of dissent being responded to with change, creating further dissent. The frustration created by this circular process can be seen in the various admissions from Lindelof and Cuse that fans will "never be completely happy" with what the show does. There is just no way to make everybody happy, and there is a certain segment of the fandom that seems impossible to please. Damon Lindelof calls it "the Goldilocks paradox." In his words: "The porridge is never, ever just right on *Lost*. It's always too hot or too cold. So you're moving too fast, and things get confusing, and people go: 'I can't really follow the show right now,' or you're moving too slow, and people go: 'This is

Carlton Cuse and Damon Lindelof hold court at the 2008 Comic Con *Lost* panel, sponsored by the Dharma Initiative . . . until the sponsorship was revoked halfway through the panel.

frustrating, they're stalling and I'm not getting any answers to my questions.'" These "people" are the fans. And Lindelof knows that the audience has this bipolar reaction to the show because he has taken the time and made the effort to suss out what the fans are thinking — to the point of accepting the limitations of what he as the show's co-creator and co-showrunner can fully promise to said audience.

One of the biggest fan complaints during the first two seasons was regarding the reruns. *Lost* never had more repeats than any other show on television, but the sense of urgency that comes with its mystical mysteries created a perspective amongst fans that the story was somehow being harmed by the stops and jerks in the narrative flow. The common complaint was that every time the show seemed to be finding its optimal rhythm, a string of repeats would pop up to banish the groove to a land of grating syncopation. And then the "explanations."

Lost's face men, Cuse and Lindelof, and ABC's Stephen McPherson were frequently defending the repeats by explaining the "sweeps" process that has been the cornerstone of television advertising marketing. But there was a problem. The "sweeps" way of doing business was woefully antiquated, a relic of a bygone era, and in the world of instant gratification and customization, the consumer's drive to have things fit their own needs would not be denied.

One of the main arguments against the "sweeps excuse" was the FOX show *24*, which had become enormously successful before the arrival of *Lost* thanks to the show's trademark of both being a serial and having a no-repeats airplay schedule. The comparison itself was not enough to build a valid argument, but the findings of fans who were not content to simply accept the "sweeps" explanation may have been.

Under closer scrutiny, fans began to understand that the "sweeps" way of airing programming was a pre–information age relic that could arguably serve better as a display of network disingenuousness than any legitimate need to do business in the present. In the days before instant communication 24/7, coast to coast, via the Internet, the Nielsen families would keep diaries of their TV viewing, and the diaries would later be collated by Nielsen and used to establish the ratings factors that we know today. The purpose of "sweeps," in that age, was to load the schedules with sprints of original, highly promoted programming, and to sell the spoils of that period as if they represented the average season-wide numbers.

With next-day reporting, these kinds of tactics wouldn't fool an advertiser, and they wouldn't convince fans who were tired of reruns either.

Whether it was the proliferation of more enlightened discussions that eventually caused the end of *Lost*'s reruns or not, the change itself proved to be destructive in a few ways. Shifting a show that once had a typical fall-show production schedule to a repeat-free schedule wasn't going to be easy. Shortly after the decision to end the repeats was leaked, the public became obsessed with yet another talking point: when would *Lost* return to the air? If *Lost* were to air without reruns, it could not return in the fall. Suddenly the prospect of a ten-month-or-longer hiatus became a reality to *Lost* fans, and the cycle began all over again.

The pod approach (of splitting the season into two parts, see p. 165) created yet another rotation of fan distress leading to production concession leading to fan distress. No one had ever produced a podded schedule before, so there was no benchmark for doing it properly; it was an absolute experiment.

The most persistent hum of dissatisfaction from *Lost* fans, though, began at the very beginning. Whether it took the waveform of "What is the monster?" or "What did Kate do?" or "What is in the hatch?" the most persistent complaint for fans was the unwillingness of the writers to let go of the story's biggest answers. As the question-to-answer ratio grew more daunting with each episode, the idea that *Lost*'s writers were being evasive became less of a knee-jerk assertion and more of a certainty. The generic explanation, that *Lost* was a self-contained story and without an end date it was difficult to judge when to give answers, made sense. But it also generated a new complaint and concern: if *Lost* were stretched too far, would it eventually fade from the airwaves as transparent wisps of the solid form it was intended to be, without ever giving the answers fans seek; or would it, to its own peril, give those answers up and become

>: "And Zombie… the 'answers' special is Carlton and I making our best effort to tell the fans all of the questions we HAVE actually answered in an effort to deflect the ongoing criticism that we never give any answers. I suspect this will backfire massively, but hey, we have to try."
— Damon Lindelof, 5/3/07

>: "…as far as jack's dad marching around, well, that falls under the category of things for which there are many possible answers, like the mysterious appearances of walt? is it possible that somewhere on the island walt and the monster are sitting around saying 'has anyone seen that jerk christian shephard? he owes me six bucks!' well… possibly (if unlikely) but frankly, a lot of the metaphysical things will probably remain shrouded in ambiguity for the foreseeable future."
— Javier Grillo-Marxuach, 10/20/05

>: "My What: who's to say we're not doing a show about time travel right now?"
— J.J. Abrams, 11/4/04

>: "Time travel. Hmmmm. Interesting."
— Damon Lindelof, 11/4/04

(All quotations from TheFuselage.com)

something it was never intended to be, trivializing those treasured reveals along the way?

In what could either be confirmation of the producers understanding of the weight of a unified fan scene, or a highly detailed illusion of that very same thing, producers Damon Lindelof and Carlton Cuse echoed the fan scene's frustration with the slowly advancing plot. The duo had chosen to negotiate for an end point, but not in traditional behind-closed-doors meetings. Their goal to bring the series to an end on their own terms was repeated over and over again through various radio interviews and press events. Along with the general desire to bring the show to a satisfying end was the dread-filled prediction that unless ABC made the decision, ending the show on good terms would eventually become impossible. Damon and Carlton had clearly learned that the fan scene's own organic tendency to develop density around a production philosophy, story line or casting choice, could have value in the boardroom as well. Or could it?

The groundwork for this campaign was laid down in season 2, though it was probably not intentional at the time. In that season, Damon and Carlton took possession of the reins of *Lost* and made it clear to everyone that they were the de facto pilots "flying the plane" (see p. 55) known as *Lost*. They began churning out official podcasts and took control of statements coming from the Writers' Room, including the bold decision at the end of season 3 to go into "radio silence" — insuring that no one made any statements to the press or even less official media outlets with regards to the season 3 finale or to what lay in store for *Lost* fans in season 4. While at the end of season 1, it was uncertain who was making the important decisions with regards to the roadmap for the show, by the end of season 3, the fans knew without a doubt that it was Damon and Carlton. So, when interviews they gave during season 3 began including discussions of *Lost* ending around 100 episodes, the fans noticed. When Damon and Carlton said that it was not really up to them — they could leave when they felt the show was done, but ABC could always hire new showrunners to play out the mysteries of the show for years — the fans championed the current showrunners and were already protesting the possibility of anyone but Damon and Carlton being allowed to bring *Lost* to its intended conclusion. Subtly, Damon and Carlton were campaigning in anticipation of a meeting with the suits that they knew was going to happen soon, and they were hoping that the popular vote of the fans would garner influence in the negotiations.

Whether their comments to the press were strategically planned or amazingly apropos in their coincidence, they seem to have gotten the desired outcome: Damon and Carlton negotiated and received an end to *Lost* with the network, an unprecedented three seasons down the road. Not only that, they also contracted the exact number of episodes for each remaining season, 16, and that each season from 4 through 6 would be shown in the spring, back to back, from beginning to end, with no repeats.

Lost is not the first show to air its episodes in this fashion. As mentioned earlier in this chapter, *24* made this method their standard. The difference is that season 2 of *Lost* was aired, then the schedule was changed for season 3, and then changed again for the remaining seasons, and this can directly be attributed to how the fans reacted to each reincarnation.

How much fan involvement is too much when it comes to running a television show? With traditional news outlets being trumped by renegade bloggers for the *real* news on everything from who's joining/leaving a show to a detailed synopsis of a supposedly top secret season finale, the television (and movie) industry has had to venture outside the typical avenues for interacting with their audience. If fans aren't happy with an episode that airs on a Tuesday night, the showrunners and network heads are aware of the unhappiness by Wednesday morning via bloggers and message boards. The fans of *Jericho* sent thousands of pounds of peanuts to save their show, but it was only saved for one season and still did not manage to garner a large enough audience to satisfy the network. There is a difference between listening to your fans and listening to your most vocal fans. *Lost* has not quite discovered the secret to managing this tricky balance, but through staying as close to their fanbase as possible — via keeping abreast of happenings and discussions on The Fuselage and other *Lost* forums and blogs — they have managed to turn the tide. Without completely giving in to fan sentiment, the showrunners and the network executives have managed to address the largest complaints — too many repeats, scheduling, lack of answers, no end in sight — while keeping their vision for the show intact.

In true "be careful what you wish for" fashion, seasons 4 through 6 of *Lost* are intended to be shown in 16 episode clumps, with no planned breaks or repeats, because that's what the fans wanted. Did they also want the eight-to-nine-month break that this arrangement will require? No. But it is undeniably the only way this schedule could happen. As much as the fans abhorred the extended hiatus, they hated the repeats and mini-pods even more. From the reaction to season 4, it appears that the added time to make the episodes, the definitive end date, and adopting *24*'s style of airing episodes of *Lost* was a good call. The show is better than ever, which makes the fans happy.

PART 3

Chapter 14

BUILDING
(AND BREAKING)
THE FOURTH WALL

BY THE TIME *Lost*'s second season was underway, the series had a reputation as not only a cerebral viewing experience, but a show that had generated a substantial think tank of online fans. While most of the work done in exploring *Lost*'s tertiary story elements — rich dissertations on the books, songs, philosophers and symbols referenced in the show — was as ancillary to the show as you could get, it was clear that the Internet scene was ripe for its own immersive experience.

How did "The Lost Experience" come to be? The answers vary. The concept of an alternate reality game has been around for some time. ARGs are role-playing games that take place primarily on the Internet, their distinguishing characteristic being that they insert the player into the actual world of the game. Players often interact with characters through message boards or by becoming privy to the characters' communications via video drops or blogs. The players in the game generally try to consciously extend the artifice of the game's constructs for mutual benefit.

The dedication of players is so impressive, and the popularity so viral, that ARGs have rapidly become a potent marketing tool. An ARG of sorts, more of a virtual docudrama, is credited for the success of *The Blair Witch Project*, and the ARG model has become an integral part of the release of the *Halo* series of video games.

The *Lost* fan scene was probably the best market to dump an ARG on at the time. *Lost* fans' ability to work out complex puzzles was already proven, as was their desire to tirelessly dig for the smallest clues. The scene was equipped not only with the ability to work through anything the creators could throw at them, but the demonstrated tenacity to follow it through to the end.

The project, The Lost Experience (TLE), was conceived in the L.A. offices, where Damon Lindelof and Carlton Cuse guided the initial concept, eventually passing the reins to Javier Grillo-Marxuach and Jordan Rosenberg. Sponsorship was spread between ABC, Channel 7 in Australia, Channel 4 in the UK and a cabal of 16 other smaller networks worldwide. Outside funding came from commercial ventures such as Sprite, Jeep and Verizon. It would later be a common complaint that the commercial elements detracted from the focus of the game.

The plan involved a story built around a central protagonist, Rachel Blake, who was out to expose the diabolical secrets of the Hanso Foundation. True to the ARG model, the game took place in our universe. As such, the show *Lost* was a component of the game's "playing field" and would be regarded as a propaganda machine being used by the Hanso Foundation to cover up their experiments.

Telling the story would involve a mixture of several websites linked together by a succession of online clues, with further information available in the form of television commercials, voicemail systems, faux interviews with fictional author Gary Troup (who also wrote the oft-mocked *Lost* pseudo-fiction *Bad Twin*) and even the commercial websites of the sponsors (who were no doubt guaranteed suitably visible intersects into the world of the game).

Helping to guide the gameplay and keep players from falling through the cracks were a collection of full-time bloggers with an inside track on the ARG. The team of Speaker (Andy Floyd) from the U.S.A., The Lost Ninja (Tom Ragg) from Australia and The Other Girl from the UK provided running commentary and more than a few helpful nudges in the right direction when necessary. These tour guides of the nebulous *Lost* Experience world weren't merely paid help, though, they were the same type of true-blue fans the creators would expect to be playing the game.

Andy Floyd reminisced about being asked to join up with the project: "I started a fan club for a great man by the name of Javier Grillo-Marxuach, and at the time he was one of those staff writer producer types on the show. His time on staff was winding down right before TLE; he was getting ready to move on. And TLE was sort of his last big gift to *Lost*. So, one day before I had even heard *Lost* was looking into Internet games, I get a call from Javi asking me if I want to be a part of a *Lost* . . . thing. I said, 'SURE!' He warned me, 'Before you say yes, realize you won't be getting paid — you'll be doing this out of the goodness of your heart.' Of course, I laughed and said, 'Don't worry, I know what I'm getting into!' Famous last words."

With the creative end sewn up, and the financial side of things shaping up, the team went about creating the bits and pieces that would serve as the "tokens" of gameplay to support the more elaborate narrative. Production of the video elements were managed, naturally, by the tendrils of the production office, while the online elements went to development house Hi-ReS!, who had created the first *Lost*-based ARG of sorts for the Channel 4 site, "Lost: The Untold." The often eerie treasure hunt–themed game was produced to help support marketing efforts for the British release of *Lost*, but had become a fan favorite internationally as well. With everything ready to go, it was just a matter of waiting for the Dungeon Master to roll the dice.

Early gameplay was scattered. Arguably, the first indication that something was going on was the disappearance of the Hanso Foundation website. The site had been running for some time and was thought to be a network-owned website. The site had become a bit of a frustration for clue-seeking fans. Hanso was known from the show as the financial backbone of the Dharma Initiative, but the site had little connection to the Dharma Initiative despite listing some compelling projects of Dharma-like proportions, including psychological experimentation and life extensions. Curiously, the site contained a project related to contacting extraterrestrial intelligence, and another project with the conspicuous acronym of J.E.D.I. These were removed prior to the site being prepped for the game.

The watchwords were given later via the official podcast when Lindelof

and Cuse described the site as being down for improvements. As rumors cir-
culated, fans became increasingly vigilant, watching for signs of the game's
development.

As a testament to the sort of frothing-at-the-gate that built up over the
game's release, word quickly spread that the first phase of TLE, a television commercial with a telephone number leading to the Hanso Foundation's hacked
PBX (or telephone switchboard), had appeared on the British airwaves. Though
the game was originally intended to be a phased worldwide release, fans braved
international long-distance rates to get the game's first clues. As the transcrip-
tions of the voice messages hidden throughout the system made their way
around the Internet, the new version of the Hanso Foundation website went
live and the game's hero was revealed.

A conspiracy is afoot! Why else would Rachel Blake, Speaker and DJ Dan from The
Lost Experience be caught cavorting? Well, in this case, they are just hanging out at
Bowlapalooza 3 as their real life alter-egos: Jamie Silberhartz, Andy Floyd and
Javier Grillo-Marxuach, respectively. Hanso can sleep easy tonight.

In keeping with *Lost*'s conventions of mythic reference, The Lost Experience's protagonist was a character named Persephone. While scholars groaned over the persistent mispronunciation of her handle as "Purse-a-phone" (it's purse-EF-innie) by the players of the game, the character went about her plan to expose the inner evils of the Hanso Foundation. Initially, the skilled hacker's revelations were scattered about the Hanso site in a sort of hide-and-seek fashion, occasionally

>: "nedh — dharma industries? news to me — you will have to tune in tonight for some real scoop behind the dharma initiative."
— Javier Grillo-Marxuach, 10/5/05

>: "Death — Wow! I've never had a minion before. Is that like… a really small onion?"
— Damon Lindelof, 11/4/04

>: "The greatest thing about working on Lost? Is watching Damon walk around the office all day, drinking martinis with cocktail minions in the glass."
— J.J. Abrams, 11/4/04

(All quotations from TheFuselage.com)

requiring a code that could be found on any one of the commercially sponsored tie-in sites.

During the latter first phase of the game, Persephone found an ally in the radio personality of DJ Dan, a sort of Captain Midnight incarnation of Art Bell, performed by Javi Grillo-Marxuach himself.

To use a popular Carlton Cuse metaphor, part one of the Experience was very much like a mosaic. Hidden across the various sites, videos and faux radio shows were tiles of knowledge that indicated a larger picture, but seemed to hold little narrative of their own. It wasn't until the second stage of the game that the actual narrative was revealed.

The Hanso Foundation website was shut down and in the process a new blog popped up. Enter Rachel Blake. The perky adventuress had a lot in common with Persephone, particularly in her quest to learn more about the dealings of the Hanso Foundation, but the arrival of this persona seemed to finally bring a flow to the story line. Rachel Blake did not have a particular inkling as to what was going on at the Hanso Foundation, just that something sinister existed within the halls of the organization. A mysterious figure named Thomas Mittelwerk had wrested control of the foundation away from its founder and namesake who had himself seemingly vanished. Meanwhile, there were indications of a bizarre plot to kidnap mathematical savants in order to solve the mysterious "Valenzetti Equation."

As Rachel pursued Mittelwerk in her quest for truth, players were constantly fed red herrings that seemed to indicate a connection with the island and elements of *Lost* itself. These connections where shattered when the game took a nearly metafictional twist at the San Diego Comic Con where Rachel Blake showed up in character to confront the cast and crew. After admonishing them for contributing to a cover-up, Blake revealed the next phase of the game, a website called stophanso.com.

The Stop Hanso and subsequent Apollo Candy bar–sponsored "Where's Alvar" sections of the game were considered the most tedious. Stop Hanso tasked fans with locating "glyph" codes. The glyphs were spread everywhere from fansites, to official *Lost* sites, to physical locations such as office doors and billboards. Each code unlocked a segment of video filmed by Rachel. ABC marketing had promised a reveal to the meaning of the infamous *Lost* numbers 4 8 15 16 23 42, at this phase but critics charged that the use of the numbers in this video were merely another inexplicable appearance of them.

In the video, Mittelwerk lectures team members on the protocol involving the release of a deadly virus. The intent would be to influence the numbers, which are factors that predict the end of mankind. The theory is, alter a factor and you could put off the extinction of the human race. Or at least delay it. Mittelwerk uses a Dharma Initiative orientation-style video featuring Alvar Hanso to back up his thesis.

There has been tremendous debate over whether the characters, films or mythology of The Lost Experience should be considered canon. There are several well-thought-out theories that use the events and ideas of The Lost Experience in tandem with events of the show. Since the show exists as a work of fiction within the universe of the game, the argument that the Dharma and even Hanso of the game are different from their "fictional" counterparts found in the show. Indeed, to include Rachel Blake and Mittelwerk within the *Lost* universe, you would also have to include the creators and cast, via the Comic Con element.

The tedious glyph hunt ended with the reveal of Mittelwerk's plan, and some tantalizing background on the infamous numbers of *Lost*, but fans were not feeling the conclusion. The general consensus was that the glyph hunt was, while ingenious in the beginning, a bit of a buzzkill in comparison to the intricate plotting that preceded it.

As far as the resolution to the story itself goes, The Lost Experience plays very much like an episode of *Lost*. Rachel Blake, like most heroes in the *Lost* universe, is not necessarily primarily concerned about the axis of her story. Just as the island is the way station in most of the characters' stories of redemption, Rachel Blake is navigating the mysteries of Dharma, Valenzetti and Mittelwerk to resolve a personal quest — to uncover the reason why Alvar Hanso has been secretly funding a trust for her. In a moment worthy of "Luke, I am your father," the mysterious Hanso admits to Rachel that he is, well, her father and gives her on-tape testimony of Mittelwerk's diabolical plot so his progeny can thwart the demented scientist.

The game ended with a live DJ Dan show featuring fan call-ins — the second DJ Dan to feature live, well-behaved fan interaction — and an in-studio chat with Rachel Blake, played by Jamie Silberhartz. During the show, Mittelwerk's arrest was simulcast but when the G-men arrived to take him away they were greeted by a bomb. The implication being that Mittelwerk was still "out there" looking for another opportunity to put his plan in motion.

The creators initially assured fans that there would not be a second Lost Experience during the gap between seasons 3 and 4, and they were true to their word. In the weeks leading to the buildup for season 4, however, a number of mysterious commercials, websites and voicemail systems began to spring up again. This time, it was Oceanic Airlines at the center of the plot. The new experience, titled Find 815, would serve as a literal prologue to the fourth season of *Lost*.

A far more self-contained story, Find 815 was viewed by players as more of an interactive episode. In fact, the episode featured over 40 minutes of video clips that comprised the "narrative" of the story, and any of the tasks, clues and games related to unlocking these pieces are truly secondary to understanding the "story" of Find 815. The launch of the game found some familiar faces returning to the blogging world, like Speaker and The Lost Ninja, and the accessibility of the game, its straightforward approach and narrow corridor proved a more pleasing platform for fans.

The story was of an Oceanic employee named Sam whose girlfriend Sonya was a flight attendant on Oceanic 815. This time, known characters such as Charles Widmore were mentioned in passing.

When *Lost* finally returned, however, some fans were outraged to learn that the events of the game were, again, not canonized by the series. Lindelof and Cuse have since refined their answer to the question of tangential products place in the *Lost*-verse by stating that they would not place information outside of the show that would be vital to understanding the story, referring to the "mothership" of the show's network-aired installments as the only pure canonical components of the *Lost* story.

A second "prologue" introduction to season 5 was launched, citing the warm reception of Find 815, with an advertisement airing during the season 4 finale directing viewers to the Octagon Global Recruiting website (www.octagonglobalrecruiting.com). A visit to the site revealed that this ARG would launch in San Diego on July 24–27, 2008 — the dates for San Diego Comic Con 2008.

Chapter 15

AMONG
THE *LOST*

By DocArzt

MY JOURNEY TO THE SET OF *LOST* BEGAN, surprisingly, at a water-cooler. Long before I was even familiar with the term "watercooler show," the watercooler was where, well, I would get a drink. Situated in a sea of cubicles inside an insidious credit card company's sprawling complex of customer service buildings, the little blue tank often served as a meeting place for weary collectors to gather and discuss "whatever," while partaking of a little hydration.

Two of my coworkers were talking about the show in excited tones, returning often to this interesting combination of indignation and anticipation over how the episode had ended. That's right; as many are surprised to learn, I was not with *Lost* from the beginning. Upon finding out that I hadn't seen it yet, which in the beginning half of the first season made you some kind of culture-less buffoon, one of them offered to bring in their Tivo box for me. At that moment I thought it was a little silly that anybody would be that excited about anything on TV. The last good shows, in my book — *Twin Peaks*, *Nowhere Man*, *The X-Files* — were long gone. But heck, when someone is so excited that they are willing to entrust you with a couple of hundred dollars of electronics you're going to at least give it the benefit of the doubt. Three days later I was not only hooked, I had found a calling.

Lost certainly does that to people. It's something I've heard over and over again since I got into this strange world of blogging about TV shows. Once you start watching you just have to know. The gravity of the show's mysteries is difficult to resist. The call to go deeper was, for me, a combination of things. First, as a writer I had tremendous respect for the show's storytelling, and what I saw as an adherence to classic storytelling devices.

I had studied under Welch Everman at the University of Maine, an author on pop-culture phenomena across the genres. It was under Welch's tutelage that I completed the process of becoming anal over the lack of "mythology" in modern-day programming. We'd often commiserate over how the promise of

Jon, his wife Charlotte and son Nick meet Michael Emerson on their set visit in Hawaii.

the *Star Wars* paradigm shift had been squandered by its countless shallow imitators. Instead of moving closer to a world of modern mythmaking, the stuffed shirts and boardrooms had reduced the moving picture — our modern equivalent of the clay tablet and story circle — to a pantomime of ever-exaggerated repetitive motions. Sadly, Welch passed away the month before *Lost* premiered.

Lost was a beacon of hope and I sought to bring my small voice to what I saw as a chorus of intelligent, thoughtful and challenging fans. I found those voices at The Fuselage. Suddenly my cynicism about the lack of good mythology was gone, along with it the sense that my craving and admiration for the art form put me in a lonely place. I became addicted to what I call "The Conversation," the amorphic but generally lofty talk that goes along with being a vocal *Lost* fan, and there I found astonishingly bright intellects.

Josh Holloway shows Nick Lachonis the "hang loose" sign.

I'm too humble to buy into the notion that I somehow gained "prominence" based on anything that I did purposefully. When I started TheTailsection. com, there was plenty of general news stuff going on, and a tad of commercialism from time to time. But for the most part, the site was my opportunity to be the guy who started "The Conversation." Every day was a challenge to, in addition to rounding up the latest stuff, craft a post that would kick things off and get people talking. The regulars came, El Prez, Captain Tripps, Erased Slate and many more, and before long the site had grown to a level that I could have never predicted.

My first exposure to the entertainment industry came earlier, though, with the exchange of thick theory-laden e-mails with *Entertainment Weekly* reporter Jeff Jensen. Before I knew it, the little blog I'd written to share my obsession with perfect strangers was among some of the highest ranking fansites in the world. Jensen shouted out to the site occasionally from his articles, as did others. The Tail Section was featured in the second issue of the official magazine. Whether I had pushed for it or not, whether my ego was aiming for it or not, the site had become a permanent fixture in the *Lost*-sphere.

The first communiqué with "insiders" came during this apex. Most were in the form of notes from mysterious people too low in the production chain to be on the credits in which they requested that I remove or retool certain items. Then I got notes from people working on the set or in postproduction. The journey towards what Erin Felentzer, in media relations at ABC, described as "Friend of the Show" was much further down the road.

My "transition" from blogger to professional journalist came with my sale of The Tail Section to BuddyTV.com. With this professional outlet, burgeoning at the time, behind me, my inhibitions began to fade, and my attempts to directly communicate with the *Lost* cast and crew became more bold. Eventually, with the help of Jeff Jensen, I was able to secure an interview with Carlton Cuse and Damon Lindelof. I can say quite honestly that I have never discussed my blogging ventures with anyone from *Lost*, and neither have they, even though we both know they exist.

Nonetheless, the first highest-level communiqué came from Carlton Cuse. A direct note thanking me for a recognition piece BuddyTV had done singling out *Lost* for bringing the most page-views to the site. I was fortunate enough to have been invited to a wedding on Oahu, one I didn't honestly expect to attend at the time, and that news brought an instant and enthusiastic invite from Cuse to visit the set.

If that seems a little too "easy" to you, I'm with you. The fact is, the invite very well could have been in part inspired by my work to energize the fans when the press was beginning to turn, my open and wide-reaching condemnation of the "ruiners" of lostfan108, or my high output of pro-*Lost* articles. Still, to this day, any mentions of those sorts of things often elicit silence from my "official" sources on the show. It's as if "DocArzt" does not exist in the same universe as "Jon Lachonis."

>: "becky — i did indeed do a commentary with carlton, maggie and ian for 'hearts and minds,' and i managed to slip the words 'hyborean' [sic] and 'tentacled buffalo monkey' into it."
— Javier Grillo-Marxuach, 7/30/05

>: "Filming is going well. I have a great scene with Foxy in Ep. 201. And I hug DOM everytime I see him and the next time will be yours."
— Jorge Garcia, 8/11/05

>: "greetings, el perdido — las cosas estan muy bien aqui en los laboratorios de lost."
— Javier Grillo-Marxuach, 10/5/05

(All quotations from TheFuselage.com)

With all of the first-person stories about how warm and fuzzy the *Lost* set is, you'd think visiting it would be the most stress-free thing in the world. That would probably be the case if you weren't a cynic, like me. Only the most naïve among us would think that everything the producers, writers and actors say about their work experience is absolutely, 100 percent true. These are people who lie for a living after all, and projecting a happy and loving set is just part of upholding the positive image of the show, right?

It was that cynicism that contributed the most to my anxiety as I weaved across the island of Oahu heading for Camp Erdman. Part of the experience was pure excitement over just being privy to some small part of the filming experience; the other was walking onto the set knowing I would be an obstacle. Sure, they will be professionals . . . but do they really want some fanboy/writer in their hair?

As we got closer to the famed camp that stood in for "New Otherton," my mind teetered between wondering who I was going to have the opportunity to talk to, and . . . why the heck are we going to New Otherton? Didn't everybody leave that place at the end of season 3?

My cell rang, Kristin the freelance publicist asked if there was any way I could get there early. Josh Holloway had to catch a flight and time was very tight. I explained I was already on the road, and Kristin warned me he may not be available due to time constraints. Great. Now I was not only the underfoot fanboy, I was also the guy who could potentially make one of the biggest stars of the show late for his flight. I will most certainly be loathed.

Jon, his Boston Red Sox cap and Jorge Garcia on location in Hawaii.

First stop on the set visit was the station known as "Base Camp." Base Camp is where a fair amount of the equipment trailers, star trailers and craft services set up. The goal with an exterior shoot, I was told, is to have this extraneous equipment as far away from shooting as is practical so to not narrow shooting opportunities. The Base Camp on this day was just outside of Dillingham Airfield. The same airfield had been used for the scenes in the Eko-centric episode "The 23rd Psalm" that explained how Eko's brother, Yemi, happened to find himself aboard the drug plane which would later show up on the island. It was also the storage space for what remained of Oceanic 815 itself.

We arrived to an empty lot. A few craft services guys were sitting under a tent talking, and a row of trailers sat like some modern effigy of the Easter Island statues overlooking the surf across the street. In the distance were the familiar buildings of New Otherton. My wife and son were allowed to come to the set as well, and I took a moment to try to goad my son into being excited about the whole thing. There was a barrier that his imagination just could not get past. The idea that anything on the television screen, including people, could exist in real life.

As I tried in vain to convince him that we were meeting real, live *Lost* folk, the door on the first trailer opened and out walked Michael Emerson in full beaten-to-a-pulp Ben Linus makeup. What would have been a very surreal moment for me was completely eclipsed by the reaction of my son who shouted "Hi Ben!", then turned, astonished, to my wife to report "Mom, Ben *is* real."

Emerson himself emitted a soft chuckle and, with a grin far removed from his sinister sneer, gave my son a finger-flowing wave that could have just as easily come from Mister Rogers.

After that, we had the pleasure of meeting Jorge Garcia in an empty parking lot, which was surely a somewhat distressing moment for him since he was equally ambushed. Then our ride arrived and we set off for where the real action was. That cynical suspicion that we would arrive on set and find ourselves in a swarm of ultra-focused type A personalities laboring over every last detail who were fighting to suppress their annoyance at our presence was back. Would I make Josh Holloway late for his plane, therefore tainting my future TV viewing experience with the thought, "There's the guy I pissed off, royally" every time Sawyer appeared on screen?

Any notion of strife on the set was erased immediately when I arrived. After getting out of the van, I noticed a rather busy-looking production worker looking at us from across the lot. Did he recognize us? How could that be? He walked enthusiastically over, a beaming smile on his face and held a hand in the air. "That's what I'm talking about!" He shouted. My first thought was, these *Lost* crew people aren't only friendly, they're a bit daft as well. He arrived at our position with his hand in the air, nodding and grinning and told me to "give it up." It slowly dawned on me that he wanted a high five. I held up my hand and he slapped it. "Boooo-yah!" he cried, turned around and returned to work. Puzzled . . . we moved on.

The scene being filmed first was later seen at the tail end of the episode "The Other Woman." Hurley and Sawyer are playing horseshoes when they are distracted by Ben Linus, who they are surprised to see off his chains, free to roam about New Otherton after, just episodes earlier, being treated as one of the largest threats on the island.

"What the hell are you doing out?" Sawyer asks.

"Oh, Locke let me go," Ben replies nonchalantly. "See you guys at dinner."

The process of multiple takes is essentially the actors doing the same thing over and over again, but with minute differences. In this sequence, Jorge and Josh delivered the exact same lines with only variations of inflection. The director worked them through several takes from angles he had determined prior to the shoot for the sake of giving the editors some latitude in terms of construction and timing. The more alternate angles, I was told, the more the editors could play with the time dimension of the scene. Even discounting the last line, which was trimmed down to simply "see you guys at dinner," the final cut was far more compressed than the length of any of the continuous takes.

As the shooting came to a close, I braced for the procession of interview subjects, my stomach in a knot. I'd prepared questions, wadded them up, put them in my pocket and wound up changing into shorts before we left for the set. So I'd be winging it. To make matters worse, a friendly looking guy approached me with a smile on his face and said, "Going to be a lot of those in the closet tomorrow, won't there?" As enigmatic as the question was, it elicited a chorus of groans from nearby crew members. Still the only person on the set who was not in on the joke, I squirmed for a moment as they looked at me expecting me to say something. I did't have a clue. Any fear of being branded as some sort of n00b to bizarre television shooting-set customs was dodged when I saw Josh Holloway walking my way, with his patented wide smile and a friendly extended hand.

I'm not out to break the hearts of Skaters, honestly, but my first thought upon sitting across from Josh Holloway is that it is absolutely true what they say about the camera distorting the physique, and how some people are made for it. Holloway is exactly as handsome as you expect him to be, but in three dimensions he is thinner, nearly gaunt, with profound lines and deep-set frighteningly crystalline eyes. Two things were startlingly unique about the experience. The first being the new "up close" perspective on Josh Holloway, and the second being the personality and intelligence of the man.

Holloway's sense of the humanity of his character is palpable. When I ask about the battle between good and evil that rages under Sawyer's mostly unshakeable exterior, Holloway waxes like a southern Joseph Campbell. "The nature of his character has been that he's constantly battling the good in him versus what he's learned as a defense mechanism in the world, which is his evil side. This whole character's journey has been a journey to his humanity, I feel like, but he has big slips."

As far as his character's transformation from the diabolical conman to the good-guy with the dark underbelly, Holloway had more introspective thoughts. "I think, in his own psyche and his whole makeup, he's trying to not go to the dark side. It's that fine line constantly with his character, and I think he scares himself sometimes. This time, on the outside, he's not showing that he cares about that or other people's judgments, but he does, and he realized he over-stepped something within himself. That's gonna take some working out, and hopefully he won't go fully to the dark side, but we'll see. I'm open, whichever way they want to go, it's just fun to walk the line. I love walking the line."

Despite the visible anxiety over making their flight, Holloway and his wife Yessica took a few minutes out to discuss my son's morally questionable choice of Sawyer as a role model. He graciously signed my son's Sawyer figure and instructed him on the proper disposal of it. "If you're anything like I was, when you turn sixteen you're going to start taking your old action figures out and blowing them up with fire-crackers. Do me a favor . . . when it comes my turn, use an M80."

I still don't know if he made that flight in time.

Next up was Jorge Garcia. Jorge was a soft-spoken, intelligent soul not at all like his on-screen counterpart. There are, no doubt, times when that is not true, and it isn't meant as an insult either way, but Garcia's relaxed, pensive approach to talking on the recorder was decidedly different from Hurley's somewhat off-the-cuff nature.

When I asked Jorge if the environment is as welcoming now as it was two seasons ago with the regards to new cast members, he replied, "I think so. I think it's fun when new people come and join us, because it's just new dynamics and new chemistries to form with people. It kind of keeps an actor on his toes. I guess that's something you have to ask them more than us, but I always try to make an effort to bring people along and tell them where the good places are around Hawaii to hit up. Especially 'cause they're all living out of their hotels at the start usually."

All of the characters on *Lost* have gone through transformations, and Hurley is no exception. Garcia is acutely aware of where his character has come from and gone in the game of island kismet. "Gradually I think we've seen, from season 1 all the way to the van moment, Hurley slowly kind of take responsibility, slowly start to be a leader and step up, and kind of take a more leadership role."

When he took a moment to pose with my son for a snapshot, he made time to teach him the popular hang-loose or "shaka" sign. Garcia has clearly gone native. I asked him if it has settled in yet that the show is ending after two more rounds of filming and much like the characters on the show, he too will be compelled to leave the island. He has. "I'd been house hunting, but never finding anything, so now I'm definitely looking at going back to California to be closer to the business and my family and stuff. That reality I'm dealing with. I've been in the same place for three seasons so far, so I have amassed stuff that now has to either get sold off or sent back."

Michael Emerson walked around the set with a book bag. Inside were, obviously, the script for the current episode, as well as a few other periodicals I'd love to have identified. When the camera is not rolling, Emerson is nothing like his character. Disarmingly polite and approachable, if Emerson were inhabited by the evil of Ben Linus, he would be a far more dangerous villain simply due to his social grace.

As many of the actors on *Lost* have said, in various ways, Emerson was quick to acknowledge that part of the job is all about "pretending" you know what is going on, even though the actors themselves don't have a clue. For Emerson, though, this is an artistic gift. "As far as predicting where things are going, I've long since given up on that on *Lost*. In a way it's freeing. I don't have to worry about story arc or character arc; where did I come from or where am I going? All of that is denied me, so all I have to do is really learn the lines and show up, and play the scene of the moment."

When it comes to Emerson's take on what makes Ben so sinister, he admitted it is mostly a matter of leaving the interpretation open to the fan. "I just found an interesting tension between being mild-mannered and the sort of context of the story, so I was happy. I just gave it the lightest read, and people fill in the blanks that way."

Despite that sort of "hold up a mirror" approach, Emerson knows how to summon Ben's ominous nature in the real world, on cue. When I ask him to sign my season 2 DVD set, he obliges, hissing "Of course, I'll sign it here . . . under . . . 'The Whole Truth.'"

As I was waiting around for the opportunity to speak with Elizabeth Mitchell (Juliet Burke), Emerson steps in to give her a hand in finding that "special" place they were all at during the iconic opening scene of "Tale of Two Cities." They would be filming a sequence that essentially adds a new angle to the scene where the New Otherton residents gather in the square to watch Oceanic 815 breaking up overhead. Emerson would not actually be in the scene, and no new dialogue was being recorded. But for the sake of setting the right tone,

Emerson was more than happy to help out by reciting from memory his infamous speech sending Ethan and Goodwin off the infiltrate the survivors.

In the middle of the takes, Elizabeth Mitchell seemed to be eyeballing me from afar. She had that same crazed glow that had been stalking me around the set all day long. Surely, she couldn't be . . . "one of them." But she was.

"Hey!" she yelled at me, and suddenly I'm afraid. I'd been dodging the fact that I should be in on the punch line all day long, and now the lovely Elizabeth Mitchell is going to be the one to finally flush me out. "There's another Red Sox fan! Hey Oakland! 11–7, I'm just saying!"

Suddenly it was all clear to me, I'd been wearing a Red Sox cap around the set all day long. A special little bit of *Lost* island magic. I hadn't bought the hat because I was a Red Sox fan, it just happened to be the closest hat within reach at the store. But as we *Lost* fans know quite well, everything happens for a reason.

Unfortunately, one thing that didn't happen was a chat with Elizabeth Mitchell. We stalked her around the set for an additional hour. Production supervisor Rich Sickler, a tall, thin presence with a sweeping stride and surfer-guy cool persona, had adopted my son as his personal assistant for the day, taking him on a brief tour of the various sets they had constructed, revealing even more of the artifice of film production, perhaps lost on the star-struck tyke's already blown mind.

Mitchell would, in a few hours, be available for an interview, but amazingly something my wife and I never expected would be possible was beginning to happen. While arranging to be accompanied by my wife and son, the publicists had warned me that set visits could be an arduous and boring experience. Before stepping "among the Lost," I couldn't have imagined that would be true. Three hours in, however, the humidity of the North Shore and the sudden stop to filming caused excitement to turn into pleas of "Can we go back yet?"

Would I have waited till the end of the day for a sit-down with the lovely Elizabeth Mitchell if I had to? Of course I would have. But hell hath no fury like a bored six year old, so, sadly, the day ended without any privileged peek into where Juliet was coming from, or whether or not Mitchell saw her character as a Shakespearean device (in the sense of being the "daughter" of rival families). Even in life, *Lost* will have its unanswered questions, and questions never asked.

Chapter 16

EASTER
EGGSPLOSION

FOR MOST VIEWERS OF *LOST*, the existence of what are known as "Easter eggs" in many episodes may be unknown. Some may have caught on to the frequent appearances of Hurley's lottery ticket numbers (4 8 15 16 23 42, aka "the Numbers") or noticed that characters on the show have the same names as various famous philosophers and people in the Bible, but more than likely, they never thought much past those realizations. These viewers watch the show strictly for entertainment — and they are sufficiently entertained by what occurs and what is seen in every episode. But there is a portion of the audience who take the phrase "you can't judge a book by its cover" in a very literal sense when it comes to *Lost*. To this group, there is a whole other story being told each week, along with the regular plot and story lines of the show. They are the Easter egg hunters — and the creators of *Lost* not only embrace this group, but they also go to great lengths to feed their Easter egg "addiction," so to speak.

For those of you who are not aware of what an Easter egg is, it is exactly what it sounds like, a treat that has been hidden by the "Easter Bunny" (in this case, *Lost* Labs don the bunny ears) for the viewers of *Lost* to find. For pop culture aficionados, finding one is just as exciting as finding one of those plastic eggs under the couch filled with money or chocolate. The best definition of an Easter egg, in the realm of *Lost* at least, is anything that is more than what it seems to be within a frame of film, an episode or the show as a whole — and it must be intentionally put there by the creators. It may be the repeated use of the Numbers or various character names, as mentioned above, or it could be a book Sawyer is reading, or a more literal Easter egg that is hidden in a frame of an episode and can only be seen using the frame-by-frame on your DVD or DVR. The significance and meaning of the Easter eggs are as varied as the theories about the show itself.

The repeated appearance of a number as an Easter egg is not a new concept for J.J., Burky or those other members of *Lost* Labs who previously worked on *Alias*. Throughout all five seasons of *Alias*, the number "47" was significant to the mythology of Milo Rambaldi (a Nostradamus-like figure), along with this symbol: <o>. Both the number "47" and the <o> symbol appeared many times. For habitual viewers of the show, they represented Rambaldi; for a newer fan, their inclusion was not disruptive, and knowledge of their significance was not required to enjoy the show — which is the hallmark of a true Easter egg. These Easter eggs were a kind of secret code between the creators and their die-hard fans, a wink-wink, nudge-nudge that added to the continuity of the show, as well as giving the fans a kind of side game to "play along at home."

On *Lost*, that use of Easter eggs has been taken to a level far beyond what was on *Alias*. Executive producer Bryan Burk (who was a co-producer for *Alias*) considers the Easter eggs to be a part of experiencing the show on a truly interactive level for those fans who choose to join in on the fun. When comparing the Easter eggs from the two shows, Burk states: "More so in *Lost* . . ., the Easter eggs are tied more into the actual canvas and the story line. In *Alias*, some of them were. But in *Lost*, it's definitely interwoven into the actual fabric of the show." Combine that with some of the most intelligent fans around and the advent of DVRs with frame-by-frame capabilities, and a monster has been born. For the weekly viewer, if you never catch a single Easter egg, you can still enjoy the show. That is part of the brilliance of the concept.

For fans who want to peel apart the layers of *Lost* in search of deeper meanings and long sought after answers, the Easter eggs have been a guide — egging them on, as it were.

What started as a fun way for the writers and producers to add to the viewing experience for their information-starved fans soon escalated to a level that took the creators somewhat by surprise. With so much symbolism being discovered, those already obsessed with the show found a way to channel their addiction into research at a graduate school level. Instead of one or two Easter eggs being found in an episode, there were a dozen. Nothing that appears in a scene, no dialogue is taken for granted. Everything has come under intense scrutiny — in some cases, to a point beyond what the creators had intended.

Gregg Nations, script coordinator and now co-producer and writer for *Lost* (ironically, he co-wrote the season 4 episode "Eggtown"), has taken the extra scrutiny in stride. When asked about it in his forum on The Fuselage, this was his response: "I don't get frustrated with the over analyzing — I just laugh, call the props department and say, 'I know this is silly, but watch out for the copy-right dates of what books you put on the shelves. Fans are looking them up to date the flashbacks.' Usually I get dead silence and then, 'You're kidding me.' Now those are fun conversations." He has also gone on to say that the props department and set dressers are now more aware of this group of fans who examine everything, and they are much more adept at keeping everything in a shot within the appropriate timeline. But it is impossible for them to truly catch "everything," so Nations occasionally has to admit to prop or set-dressing errors — sometimes after a dozen different theories have already sprung up on the discussion boards based on what was an unintentional mistake.

As cool as some of the Easter eggs have been, attempting to find and explain them all may take away from the enjoyment of the show, and it can cloud the viewer's judgment by encouraging constant distrust of the face-value meaning of everything in an episode. On the other hand, some of the Easter eggs have yet to even be found. As hard as it may be to believe, Burk states that some of the Easter eggs they went to great lengths, and sometimes great expense, to include have not been found by the fans. But the creators are okay with that. As he says, "It's the nature of the beast." The creators still enjoy putting the eggs in — it is part of that interactive fan experience that deepens their connection to the viewers, especially that hard-core group who compete each week to find all of the hidden eggs first.

On the other hand, sometimes a big to-do is made about something that turns out to really be nothing . . . or not much in the way of true "clues" to the many mysteries of *Lost*. One of the most recurrent visual Easter eggs has

CapnBob (the maker of the Lost Rhapsody videos)
meets Gregg Nations.

Mira Furlan played "the French Lady," Danielle Rousseau, who was responsible
for the looping radio transmission that Shannon incompletely translated in the pilot
episode. The transmission was the first Easter egg in *Lost*.

been in the form of prop books. As well, *Lost*'s characters are frequently enacting the world-views or fictional worlds of the various authors that float around in the margins of the show: John Locke, Austen, Faraday, Rousseau, and Hume, to name just a few. Seeing Sawyer reading *Watership Down* or Ben being offered a copy of *The Brothers Karamazov* gets the theorists' tongues wagging. These occasionally convoluted theories have a tendency to ignore repeated promises from the producers that there is no "hidden message" or extracurricular homework needed to understand the story of *Lost*.

A classic example of such a reference turning out to be much less than it was made out to be was Flann O'Brien's cryptic second novel *The Third Policeman*. Amongst other

>: "BTW, Anyone with HDTV got a special surprise in Charlie's second dream tonight… right when the dove appears. Hope some of you caught it — 'cause it's IMPORTANT."
— Damon Lindelof, 1/26/06

>: "OH Loyal Friends, How I love thee. Was Harold not genius in tonite's episode? I know a lot of the Fuselage fun is dedicated to finding various easter eggs (What's this Dharma business anyway?), but let us not forget to stop and appreciate what makes it all TICK."
— Damon Lindelof, 9/29/05

>: "The road is long, friends, but hopefully, when at last you reach your destination, you'll look back and remember having enjoyed the journey even more than where you ended up. And check out the milk carton. Hugs, The Blamee."
— Damon Lindelof, 10/13/05

(All quotations from TheFuselage.com)

things, the book contains an underground chamber with a counter, characters who are unknowingly in an afterlife, and a magic box that can produce whatever its bearer may desire. While all of these elements have common threads in the *Lost* universe, the book was apparently suggested by supervising producer Craig Wright, and showrunners Damon Lindelof and Carlton Cuse have admitted on the official *Lost* podcast that they have never read the book, though they do know the general premise of it, which Wright had pitched to them in order to allow its inclusion into the *Lost* universe. Wright later confessed in a radio interview with Ireland's Spin 1038 that the purpose of placing the book was to play against fans' persistent belief that the Oceanic 815 survivors were in purgatory, not to lay ground rules for "solving" the show in advance. Prior to this admission, however, the presence of the book was heralded as "ammunition" for understanding the show's mysteries. In the overall *Lost* landscape, it seems to be not much more than a gratuitously interesting knick-knack.

Why go to so much trouble to include the Easter eggs, especially considering that we know a very small percentage of the fans will be picking the episodes apart at that level? For one, "*Lost* Easter eggs" are second only to "*Lost* spoilers" when it comes to what *Lost* fans online are searching for every week after an episode has aired. What it really comes down to is this group of Easter egg–loving fans who have embraced the show on a much deeper level. For those fans and the creators, it's part of the fun. The creators appreciate the fans' unusual dedication, so it is only natural for them to want to reward it.

The first true *Lost* Easter egg, according to Burk, occurred in the pilot episode. The Easter egg is not visual, it is spoken. It is Rousseau's transmission that was picked up over the transceiver — Shannon did not translate it correctly. "The French Woman," who we later learn is Danielle Rousseau, mentions the "Black Rock," but Shannon did not translate that part. For anyone watching who spoke French and for those who went online and found the full translation, this extra piece of information did not seem significant — until later, in episode 1.06, when we met Rousseau and she mentions the Black Rock (in English this time). For most of the audience, this was something new, but for that small group who had understood the French or read the translation online, it was an exciting validation. They were right! These fans felt like they had discovered a secret treasure in the pilot episode that played out five episodes later. And by the end of the season, we actually see the Black Rock — so that Easter egg came full circle. Burk says, "To end the season when they actually get to the Black Rock — it's even more rewarding, because . . . in the last episode you discover the Black Rock, and in the first episode you heard about it. And it becomes that whole big wonderful thing where you're in on kind of the discovery, and it's what's fun. It's really what makes it interactive."

Some within the fandom feel that the Easter egg hunting is a waste of time. Is there any intrinsic value to watching Karl's brainwashing video in episode 3.07, "Not in Portland," frame by frame, then spending hours or even days developing theories based on what you discover? For many fans, the answer to this question is unequivocally "no." These same detractors will come into a theory thread or onto the LB of The Fuselage and call the dedicated theorists "crackpots" and tell them that they all "need to get a life!" For the most part, those kinds of comments get ignored and the theorists chug along full steam ahead. This is an argument that most fans feel will never be resolved — so a truce is formed by agreeing to disagree.

Lost is laying the foundation for a legacy. Imagine how much fun it will be to pull out your Lost DVDs for your kids and grandkids, then watch them go wild the first time they see the Dharma symbol on the underbelly of the shark. The layers of Lost, from its plotlines to its Easter eggs, will be picked apart by new generations of fans for years to come.

Chapter 17

A LONG TIME AGO, ON AN ISLAND FAR, FAR AWAY

WE'VE TALKED ABOUT the possibility of *Lost* being influenced by Joseph Campbell's "Hero's Journey" (see page 42), but what are the odds that the transference of Campbell's sensibilities came through another source, one that originates in a galaxy far, far away?

The connection between Campbell and *Lost* may not be in *Lost* at all, but in *Star Wars*. In an effort to explain the popularity of *Star Wars*, many film scholars and literary pundits reached for Campbell's work on *The Hero's Journey*. In Lucas's film, Campbell had found a standing testament to his dissertation on the functionality of myth. *Star Wars* worked, Campbell said, because it appealed to an unconscious need to be told just such a story in just such a way. As many star-struck writers have learned since, in trying to craft their own epics around Campbell's observations, there is far more to succeeding than merely following his general outlines. Campbell would be quick to point out that the Sumerians who carved "Gilgamesh" into stone 5000 years ago did so without a copy of his *Hero's Journey* at their side. Sometimes, great myths just happen.

Part of *Lost*'s appeal lies in the fact that it is sort of a perfect balance of sensibilities built from archetypal myth stories. J.J. Abrams said that when he first saw Damon Lindelof he knew they were going to click. Why? Because of his vintage *Star Wars* "Bantha Tracks" T-shirt. Whether the implication was that Abrams and Lindelof recognized each other as wielders of mythic archetypes is another matter altogether. That they were children of the *Star Wars* age is certain. The influence of *Star Wars* exists as a well-executed homage at various levels of *Lost*'s story. In straight point-by-point comparisons, you have a Han Solo–type character (Sawyer), an Obi Wan–style spiritualist (John Locke), a tough damsel (Kate), a R2D2-and-C3PO–type combo (Charlie and Hurley), journeys of redemption and more.

The story of *Star Wars*' influence on *Lost* doesn't end there. If you were to ask Damon Lindelof if *Star Wars* was present in his day-to-day work on the show, he'd be hard pressed to say no: he has a floor-to-ceiling movie poster of the original film in his office.

Star Wars even made an interesting *Lost*-styled backstory connection between Lindelof and co-showrunner Carlton Cuse. On the official *Lost* podcast, both men recounted an event long before they met professionally in which they unknowingly shared a close encounter with George Lucas at Disneyland. There is even a picture that shows a young Cuse, Lindelof as a child and Lucas all in the same shot.

But odd turns of fate aside, the *Star Wars* influence is strong throughout the show in more ways than just simple story mechanisms. There are many nods to the space opera classic scattered throughout the dialogue, many of them in situations that could not be any more perfect for an homage.

Take season 1 for instance. When Michael and Jin are building the second raft, there is a moment that is oddly familiar. Jin is fiddling with the construction when Michael comes over shouting angrily, "No, no! This one goes there, that one goes there!" In *Star Wars: The Empire Strikes Back*, Han Solo uses virtually the same dialogue when Chewbacca is working on the Millennium Falcon. Then Sawyer — himself a very Han Solo–esque character — says, "Hey, Han, you and Chewie want to slow down a second. . . ." And speaking of *Lost* crosses, the episode the line comes from, "Exodus Part 1," aired on the same calendar date as *The Empire Strikes Back* was released in theaters. Some things are just too good to be planned.

The Han nickname for Michael was quickly dropped, but Jin's moniker of "Chewie" would last through the season 2 episode "Abandoned." As time wore on, it became increasingly dependent on Sawyer, naturally, to throw around the *Star Wars*–themed nicknames and quotations, calling Hurley "Jabba" at one point, and evoking a famous Han Solo line, "Laugh it up, fuzzball," in response to Sayid's chuckling by saying, "Laugh it up, Mohammad."

The season 4 episode "Meet Kevin Johnson" contained one of the more infamous quotations from *Star Wars* used in its most literal way. At the end, as Danielle, Alex and Karl are unknowingly being stalked by Charles Widmore's wetworks team, Karl utters the classic *Star Wars* line "I have a bad feeling about this." His "bad feeling" turns out to be a harbinger of death. The line itself is famous for having been uttered by a variety of *Star Wars* characters in each one of the series' six films.

Of course, some may find the *Lost* crew's love of *Star Wars* predict-

>: "And yes, the Han/Chewie thing was intentional… and Sawyer points it out next week! Just a little tidbit for the midnite faithful…"
— Damon Lindelof, 5/19/05

>: "Yes they're really into Star Wars in the writers' room."
— Jorge Garcia, 7/21/06

>: "The triangle has been in place since the beginning. If you think about it, I'm sure you can figure out a similar triangle that started the same way. (Han, Luke and Leia? Lucas just chickened out and made Luke and Leia brother and sister so he didn't have to deal with the triangle thing… or the incest thing. That would've been really weird.)"
— Gregg Nations, 3/5/07

(All quotations from TheFuselage.com)

able — it is, after all, one of the most popular franchises in film history, but the impact of the movies on the show seems far deeper than the occasional shoutout.

The "stakes" of the two worlds, particularly from a character perspective, are very similar in tone and construct. The concept of a light and dark side, for one, is a clear channeling of the central motif of the *Star Wars* saga. The choice being a trip down a mystical path (magic), or a path of reason (science), is the deviation. The existence of the choice is the simile. John Locke's early reference to "sides" in the series reverberated with the elderly Obi-Wan's instruction to young Luke. While Walt does not end up in the Luke Skywalker role of the show, he does take up instruction in the art of blades with Locke acting as Obi-Wan.

The character archetypes of damsels in distress, lusty scoundrels and naïve souls on the verge of worldview-shattering shifts of perspective are not strictly the domain of *Star Wars*, but were certainly reenergized in Lucas's rendition. Likewise, *Lost*'s use of *Star Wars*–like archetypes is not merely the writers channeling the motifs of a classic for empty gain. *Lost* has, in many ways, expanded on the themes and personas that guaranteed *Star Wars* its legacy, and has, in the process, secured its own place in the universe.

Another undeniable stylistic link between *Lost* and *Star Wars* is the visual styling. Lucas was insistent on a visual design that depicted a lived-in universe. Technology in *Star Wars* is worn, rusted, banged up. *Star Wars* represented locales that looked lived-in, bringing a layer of realism that had been overlooked in its more techno-oriented contemporaries. There was plenty of gloss, too, but *Star Wars*' depiction of "used" technology was part of what seemed to

J.J. and Damon share a love of Star Wars and geek chic glasses.

push viewers through the ceiling of suspension of disbelief.

For the remains of the Dharma Initiative, *Lost* summoned the same sort of visual effect for the viewers. Dharma, despite its technology, looks ancient. The stations show the wear of those jumpsuited scientists. Yet, there is a chilling anachronistic quality to the Dharma sets; they seem more "future" than "past," despite their worn look. Like the worn-out and used technology of *Star Wars*, the Dharma technology appears strangely believable.

The creators of *Lost* don't duck their connection to the StarWarsverse. Some of the most intensive comparisons of *Lost* and *Star Wars* can be found on the official

Burky and Damon talk over each other at the official *Lost* convention.

StarWars.com website, which includes many quotes directly from the creators of *Lost*. Amongst them is J.J. enthusing about how great a literal collision of the universes would be: "I think it would be incredibly cool if the group came to a clearing in the jungle and Jabba the Hutt was sitting there. I would *love* to see that episode."

Vague and original spirituality is another component familiar to the *Star Wars* franchise. The island certainly represents a force, and one that, so far, transcends the trappings of any conventional religion. Of particular interest in our *Star Wars* comparison is the fact that a great deal of the island's "power" manifests itself as an unseen force that seems to course through everything, capable of great miracles (Locke's "cure") and horrible distortions (the smoke monster).

Furthermore, the "force" of the island seems to have no active intent. Scholars of the show have long pointed out that the island tends to react in response to the actions of those who inhabit it. Nikki, for instance, summoned her own spiders. Eko summoned the visage of Yemi just before his own death because, if you buy the pop psychology, his Catholic faith instilled a need for punishment as well as repentance. Visions of hope and dread on the island tend to coalesce based on what is in the eye and heart of the beholder. Much as the "dark side" of the force is a manipulation of a neutral quantum, the dark side of the island seems also to be driven by an inner darkness left unchecked.

Along with the more visceral introductions of the island's oblique spirituality are the general metaphors. The characters of *Lost*, like those of *Star Wars*, are constantly being guarded by some oppressive force looming over their decisions to choose one path or another. Every move has the dire, inexorable momentum of the same kinds of movements in *Star Wars*. Do you go with the others, or return to your people? Do you make the run against the Death Star despite overwhelming odds? Do you infiltrate New Otherton despite overwhelming odds? *The Millennium Falcon* (which made an Easter egg–ish appearance in the episode "Something Nice Back Home" as one of young Aaron's cooler toys) is a hulking clunker that sweeps in at the last moment to save the day and turn the tables. Hurley's vw van, a hulking clunker, sweeps in at the last moment to save the day and turn the tables.

Whether it is cheeky quotations, stylistic sensibility or even out-and-out plot mechanisms, there seems to be an oversized *Star Wars* heart pumping at the center of *Lost*. Despite this, what is cosmically clear is that the writers on *Lost* are not relying on the beaten paths of *Star Wars* to guarantee the show's own legacy. *Lost* is merely paying tribute on its way to its own place on the tapestry of pop culture.

Chapter 18

ATTACK OF
THE PODS

THROUGHOUT THE FIRST TWO seasons of *Lost*, the fans made it clear that they hated the reruns. There seemed to be no rhyme or reason as to when ABC aired a new episode and when it ran a repeat. The blocks of episodes without interruptions or repeats (Damon Lindelof refers to them as "pods") were getting shorter, while the blocks of repeats were getting longer. The frustration of the fans was palpable — Damon even addressed the problem during his visits to The Fuselage. In late March 2006, amidst the confusing season 2 airing schedule, he posted this to the fans there:

> To the loyal fans, I thank you for hanging in. We've pushed to do FOUR new eps in this pod (instead of the original THREE) just to fight off the haters . . . but alas, what can we do? We have 24 hours and 36 weeks in which to air them. It sucks. And no one hates it more than we do.

It was the combination of fan complaints and the producers' desire to air the show in the best way for serialized storytelling — by running the episodes back to back — that led to the decision to try something different for season

hijinx, katejones, q and Carencey show off their "Blame Damon" shirts. When a *Lost* episode completely blows your mind, feel free to blame Damon along with the rest of us.

3. There would be no reruns.

The end of repeats brought new challenges for the *Lost* producers, as well as the network. In order for the show to remain truly repeat-free, the creators would need to complete more episodes in advance of the premiere date. That way, *Lost* could return to its typical fall season slot. The alternative: keep *Lost* fans waiting and premiere the third season mid-season, extending the show's hiatus to nine months. Before the scheduling was even confirmed, fan anxiety began to percolate up through the message boards and blogs as industry savvy fans were coming to the conclusion that a repeat-free season would mean no new *Lost* for the same amount of time it would take to conceive and deliver baby Aaron. It was understandable to wish for no reruns, but it was a shock once reality started to hit the fans . . . and the fan.

With the average episode taking somewhere in the neighborhood of ten days to shoot, and a few more weeks to edit, score, finish special effects and whatever other secret processes Bad Robot employs in completing an episode, the production would quickly bottleneck if *Lost* returned with the rest to the fall schedule.

As the Internet grapevine began to bear sour grapes, Damon Lindelof and Carlton Cuse came forward with an interesting compromise pulled from their patented creative problem-solving skills: the third season of *Lost* would be split into two "pods." The first would air from October 4 to November 8, 2006; these six episodes would encompass a single story arc designed to sketch out the playing field for season 3 proper. Then the 16 remaining episodes would be shown consecutively, beginning on February 7 and concluding on May 23, 2007.

If reaction was tame in the beginning, it was because most fans didn't know how to respond. On one hand, there was no mammoth, unbearable hiatus to languish through; on the other, a second 13-week hiatus seemed foreboding to some, bearable to others, and absolutely unacceptable to many. As the *Lost* crew had come to realize already, there was no pleasing the entire fan

Carlton Cuse in a contemplative state. He and Damon worked on the "suits" at ABC to schedule *Lost in* a way that would make the fans happier.

scene, so the uproar surely must have seemed like business as usual. But there were more hazards in this course of action that had yet to appear.

For all of the behind-closed-doors planning that went into selling the idea of cutting a major network hit like *Lost* into two pods to be released straddling an entire sweeps period, the final word on success or failure would come from the fans, and the entertainment media sat ready with knives and forks to feast on their displeasure.

Season 3 also saw the arrival of an arbitrary "line in the sand" for *Lost*. Season 2's stronger science fiction themes and the tendency to pivot between mythology and character-driven episode models had created a sort of division within the fandom. For every *Lost* fan who was in it for the ride, there was another one demanding answers, and yet another claiming the series had lost its first season "soul." For the carnivores in the vast Internet entertainment press, the negative emanations of the *Lost* scene could mean only one thing: *Lost* had "lost" it. Internet media is just like every other form of media; negativity sells, positivity is boring. Regardless of whether those fans who were unhappy with the season actually outnumbered those who were happy with it, there was enough grumbling to gain the attention of the Internet media — they smelled blood and pounced.

If there is such a thing as pre-cliché, it is using the word "lost" in any sentence meant to question the stamina of the show *Lost* or its audience. Even something like "Is *Lost* going nowhere?" seems too obvious to be considered anything other than passé. Nonetheless, before the "pod" experiment began, and shortly afterwards, the seemingly disenchanted press was enveloped in a haze of similarly snide headlines:

"Has *Lost* lost it?" — *The Guardian* in the UK, November 2006

"*Lost* has definitely 'lost' its appeal" — TV *Guide*, November 2006

"Why '*Lost*' has lost me as a viewer" — MSNBC.com, October 8, 2006

And so on. . . . Most of the complaints were a direct translation of the fan scene's frustration with the show's ubiquitous sense of mystery, and the growing accusation that the writers were "putting off" the larger answers. What the media had failed to interpret correctly was that the frustration was often a sort of ecstatic agony. *Lost* was beginning to "lose" its casual audience, but the hardened core that remained wasn't lining up for the hate parade. When Carlton Cuse was asked about the smaller audience for season 3 and whether or not he felt fans would be back for the second pod, he responded, "I think the question is 'What size audience does *Lost* deserve to have?' I think no one expected it to work and have a huge audience . . . I think there is a natural attrition due to the fact that this show requires sort of vigilant maintenance. You have to keep up with it." The media did not know what to do with this apparent acceptance

of fewer viewers, so for the most part, they ignored the showrunners' insistence that they were not going to sacrifice the audience they had for the sake of trying to win back the audience they seemed to have lost.

Bryan Burk talks with L. Scott Caldwell
at LOST Weekend 2007.

The first pod took on the task of giving viewers an unprecedented look at the world of "the Others." It was nothing short of a stunning introduction for fans who had up to that point been given only fleeting, ambiguous glimpses into the psyche of the island's mysterious caretakers. The second mission of the pod was to address the tension surrounding the Jack/Kate/Sawyer love triangle by having Kate finally make a choice. Reviews varied, from the rose colored any-*Lost*-is-good-*Lost* view, to those who felt the first pod focused too much on the trio of characters, leaving many fan favorites, who were back on the beach, with little more than cameos.

The reality is that the *Lost* crew had given fans fair warning as early as the 2006 San Diego Comic Con, where Damon Lindelof told the thousands of fans in attendance that ". . . we have an opportunity to learn more about these Other people, who they are, where they came from, why they captured Kate, Jack and Sawyer, but more importantly, this idea of telling an adventure story, and this captivity story, and that's really going to be a big piece of at least the first six episodes, the sort of mini-series event."

A common criticism was that the story of Kate, Jack and Sawyer's captivity seemed too drawn out. So far in the *Lost* story, the tale of the trio's imprisonment on Hydra island (also called

>: "Gang, Sorry to do such a quick buzz by, but wanted to thank you all for your continued fandom. We're all crossing our fingers that the strike will soon be over and we can [get] back to screwing with your collective brains."
— Damon Lindelof, 2/4/08

>: "It SUCKS that you have to wait three weeks for a new episode (it's a GOOD one, though), but that's the network workin' their mojo. We'd run 'em back to back if we could, but these things take a lot of time to get JUST right, and unfortunately, the reruns help us catch our breath a little on the post-production side of things… so hopefully you'll offer us just a teensy bit of slack."
— Damon Lindelof, 10/20/05

>: "I would write into ABC and let them know how you feel. The air order is completely up to them, and they base it off fan reaction and their perception of how the show plays."
— Gregg Nations, 5/5/07

(All quotations from TheFuselage.com)

"Bencatraz" by the fans) is the single longest contiguous chunk of plot. Prior to that, the longest definitive portion of plot was the first three episodes of season 2, which addressed the cliffhangers from the season 1 finale. The trio's incarceration was in glaring contrast to *Lost*'s usual modis operandi, and it rubbed some of the fans the wrong way.

Whether the fans thought the pods were a failure or not, the producers were ready to accept that the idea was a failed experiment. "I feel like we're a great football team that had a somewhat spotty preseason record, but now that we're playing for keeps, it's time to kick [butt] and take names," Lindelof exclaimed to *USA Today* on the eve of the show's return via the second pod. It seemed to even take the writers by surprise that, once they had established that those first six episodes needed to deal with the Kate/Sawyer/Jack story and the Others, there was not much time left for the rest of the Losties. As the second pod played out, those 16 episodes in a row seemed to appease the bulk of the naysayers, and so the mini-pod became a distant and unpleasant memory.

But this led to an interesting conundrum that had to be addressed during the summer after season 3 ended: what to do for season 4?

A 24-style plan was decided on for the rest of the series towards the end of season 3, but one more snag developed in the scheduling plan. The Writers Guild of America strike hit in the fall of 2007 and it affected the airing of *Lost* in both good and bad ways. On the one hand, it forced a five-week hiatus into what was supposed to be a "no interruptions" airing of the episodes back to back and shortened the already shrinking season from 16 episodes to 13 (though the finale was actually given a second hour at the last minute by the network). On the other hand, due to the preplanned extended hiatus between seasons 3 and 4, *Lost* premiered at a time when all of the other scripted shows were forced on hiatus because they had run out of new scripts to shoot. With its only competition being reality shows and reruns, *Lost* was able to strut its feathers — of course, this also brought the show under even more intense scrutiny from television critics who had no other shows to watch or talk about.

The WGA writers' strike saw writers from every corner of the television industry walk out of their offices and onto picket lines from November 5, 2007 to

February 12, 2008, including WGA members and *Lost* showrunners Carlton Cuse and Damon Lindelof. The reasons for the strike were solid: Hollywood was doing nothing to compensate writers for the transmission of their work in the Internet domain, and with futurists predicting that cable and satellite would give way to the Internet as the primary delivery method of programming within the next five years, the scribes were troubled. Already, Apple's iTunes and Apple TV had demonstrated growing markets for the purchase of television and movie programming, and the writers were not getting a cent.

For *Lost* fans, every day that ticked by brought the fourth season (which had been one of the most well-received seasons for the show) closer to oblivion. Talk from the top that a quick resolution would allow writers to get back to work without skipping a beat soon faded into a dwindling countdown of the number of episodes that could conceivably be produced. Already reduced to one of three 16-episode seasons, the fourth season was in danger of ending after an anti-climatic eight episodes.

During the strike, Carlton Cuse — also a member of the WGA's negotiation committee — made momentary and controversial headlines when he was nabbed by the press performing some of his producer duties on the fourth season. Cuse withdrew to the confines of the picket lines under questions about his commitment to the WGA cause. It was a challenge to many of those on the lines, the industry had shifted towards a sort of "philosopher king" hierarchy where showrunners were also the head writers, combining many of the duties of producer with those of the primary creative force, and in the process handicapping itself in the event of such things as the WGA strike.

In the end, the damage to the fourth season of *Lost* was not as bad as many had feared it would be. The season would end with five additional episodes, the two missing hours eventually being smoothed into subsequent seasons. Initially only five hours were approved, forcing Cuse and Lindelof to compress eight episodes of story, and what normally would have been a two-hour finale, into smaller chunks. The worst part for fans was that the changes to the season required a gap to cover additional production time. Without the lead time, the episodes could not be presented back to back as previously planned.

So, arguably, the fourth season was presented pod-fashion as well, with some fans sensing a palpable difference between the first half and the second, and for good reason. The season was already concise, so the post-strike episodes absolutely flew like lightening. Despite the noticeable difference, fans rejoiced. Perhaps part of this was the fear that the season would be a washout, combined with a much shorter waiting period for the subsequent episodes. Regardless, the second "pod" experience proved not only that the *Lost* machine functioned well under pressure, but that podding could work. Even if it was under duress.

Chapter 19

ALL
GOOD THINGS . . .

LOST FANS HATED being stuck with nothing but reruns and the mini-pod, but seemed content with getting a large chunk of *Lost* episodes in a row. The resolution turned out to be both an answered prayer and a nightmare for the fans. Damon Lindelof and Carlton Cuse struck a deal with ABC guaranteeing that *Lost* would not only be around for season 4, but season 5 and 6 as well; each season would consist of 16 episodes; and all 16 episodes would air back to back. Sounds great, right? Well, the nightmare part of this for the fans was that each year they would have to endure an extra-long hiatus from May to January in order to get the entire season without reruns and the dreaded mini-pod. This is the formula FOX's *24* used, the very formula fans pointed to in season 2 as one that would work for *Lost*. Be careful what you wish for.

The good news is that season 4 immediately knocked the audience out with more answers and tighter plotlines on a more consistent basis than had previously been seen on *Lost*. Having the luxury of plotting out the definitive ending of the show, knowing exactly how many seasons and episodes remained, unshackled the writers and allowed *Lost* to reinvent itself. The *Lost* fan boards have been reinvigorated, as fans dissect these answers and thrust new theories into the fandom ethos. Maybe good things do come to those who wait.

Lost will end in 2010. Who would have believed that such a definitive statement could be made in this day and television age? Many shows never get guaranteed the back nine episodes for a single season, much less three whole seasons and an end date. *Lost* had already managed to do the impossible in how quickly the show was green-lighted and was brought to the air with very few roadblocks — maybe the decision to declare its end date should not have come as such a surprise. Most fans were not aware of the rarity of the gift they had been given. But those within the industry definitely sat up and took notice. If possible, the magnifying glass has edged even closer — the level of scrutiny kicked up a notch. ABC threw caution to the wind and gave Damon Lindelof and Carlton Cuse what they had been pushing for — the ball is now firmly in *Lost* Labs' court. Success or failure will reflect directly on those charged with creating the show every week.

This was something that Damon and Carlton very much wanted — a definite end date that they could aim the rest of the series towards. The reason should be obvious: *Lost* is a serialized drama, a show that *needs* a planned and purposeful ending. To do it well and to do it right, the showrunners needed more than just a heads-up that the show was being canceled a few months beforehand. In fact, to really do it justice, to make the end of the show truly live up to the beginning and to give real closure to all of the amazing story lines, *Lost* needed more than just prior notice that an upcoming season would be the last one. Carlton admitted that this dilemma weighed heavily on them: "We were sort of stalling last season [season 3] . . . we didn't know whether the mythology we constructed had to last two more seasons or seven more seasons. And that was driving us crazy because we didn't know how fast it was going to play out." Damon and Carlton, sitting at the apex of their storytelling arc, at a place they knew would be the best place to start the downward slope, walked into negotiations with ABC fully prepared to fight for the ending of the show. Not just for themselves — not just to guarantee three more years of employment for themselves and everyone else on the show — but for the fans who had been through thick and thin, hatch implosion and purple sky, smoke monster and Nikki and Paulo. They wanted to finish the story of *Lost* on their own terms, so the fans would get the full scope of the story . . . the way that *Lost* Labs had intended it to be.

There really was no other way to end *Lost* that would have even the remotest chance of being fulfilling for the fans. The decision to take control of the show's destiny out of the hands of the network executives and put it back in the hands of the creators was maybe the greatest gift the *Lost* fans could receive. This show is not part of any existing status quo. It came together under highly unusual and probably never-to-be-duplicated circumstances. Announcing that it would be given an end date three years in the future is no precedent in Hollywood. There is a vast array of shows that once needed a planned ending to satisfy its audience but never got one (*Invasion, Reunion,* etc.). *Lost*'s planned ending will not change that. What it may do is allow showrunners and networks to consider the option of a planned exit — whenever the next great serialized drama comes along.

> >: "speaker — I thought the whispers were saying 'remember to drink your ovaltine.'"
> — Javier Grillo-Marxuach, 5/25/05
>
> >: "I am happy to be associated with a project that brings together such a collection of characters."
> — Terry O'Quinn, 6/30/05
>
> >: "And please, PLEASE, don't talk to Javi when he's online. He spends more time on The Fuselage than he does in the Writers Room."
> — J.J. Abrams, 12/13/04

(All quotations from TheFuselage.com)

When Damon and Carlton negotiated a finite end to *Lost*, they were not messing around or trying to bluff the network executives. They had a plan and intended to fully back it up, if given the opportunity. Not long after the deal was made and announced to the public, the creative team of *Lost* met to plan the end of the show. This was not their standard writers' retreat to break out the next season's story arc. This was a battle plan for the *rest* of the series. For the first time, no consideration needed to be given to the possibility of cancellation or the enigmatic "What if we only have two more seasons left? Or ten?" That was now a moot point. While in some industries an end point means being tied down or restricted, for the *Lost* writers, an end point equaled freedom. Freedom to divide the rest of the show into thirds; then break each third into sixteenths. Obviously, some flexibility was needed, but for the most part, the remainder of *Lost* has been mapped out. As Damon explained it, the end date ". . . was nothing less than the difference between not wanting to do it anymore and being thrilled to do it to the very end. It had become such an arduous task: 'How can we start working towards any of the things we've been doing for the last three years if we don't know when we get to do them?'"

Removing the uncertainty factor may turn out to be the best thing to happen to *Lost* since J.J. Abrams was introduced to Damon Lindelof. Season 4 was dynamic straight out of the box, and the expectations were exceptionally

Many a Dharma volunteer have walked this pier.

high due to the eight-month hiatus and the Writers' Guild of America strike making *Lost* practically the only show on the air offering new episodes. Even with the added scrutiny and the intense buildup, *Lost's* season 4 delivered in a way that most fans thought the show had not done since season 1. Some may want to credit the extended hiatus for giving the writers and the rest of the *Lost* creative team more time to truly sink their teeth into the new season, but the writing and shooting schedules remained basically the same as a regular season. The difference was control. The difference was *finally* knowing when the end was coming, which meant having the luxury of drawing the best map possible for getting there.

Carlton Cuse poses with Jacknkate1. Watch out Skaters: she may be pushing a Jater agenda on him.

Having an end date isn't just good for the creative team and good for the fans, it is good for the cast as well. Let's face it, *Lost* has one hell of a cast. To have that much talent and keep it squirreled away in Hawaii for the majority of the year is bound to cause some anxiety and frustration for the actors. It's one thing to be in Los Angeles working on a television series. If the show gets canceled or your character gets killed off or written off the show, you just head into your agent's office the next day and start looking for your next gig. For the actors on *Lost*, the demise of their character or of the show itself involves having to relocate back to the mainland, which can be especially difficult for the cast members, such as Matthew Fox, who have children enrolled in school in Hawaii. Some portion of the crew and the extras are originally based in Los Angeles — so they would be affected by any upheavals that might occur to the show as well.

An example of this exact situation happened during the writers' strike that took place in fall of 2007, a few months before *Lost* was due to return from its first extra-long hiatus. When production shut down on Hawaii, the actors and the crew were frozen in a bizarre form of limbo. Without knowing how long the strike would last or if there would be any additional episodes shot for season 4 of *Lost*, their choices were very limited on alternative forms of income. At least in Los Angeles the out-of-work actors, crew, writers, producers, directors and showrunners had compatriots to walk the picket lines with and gain support from. In Hawaii, everyone was much more isolated and "out of the loop."

Thankfully, the strike was resolved in time for additional episodes to be shot for season 4: instead of 8 hours, there would be 14 total. (And the strike created a positive outcome for the show: Nestor Carbonell, who plays Richard Alpert, had signed on to star in the CBS series, *Cane*, and was no longer able to remain on *Lost*. But during the strike, *Cane* was canceled, which allowed Carbonell to come back and film a few episodes for the end of the *Lost* season. Had the strike not happened, the season would have been filmed and finished, and Alpert wouldn't have appeared again.) But the uncertainties that the strike caused had to have lingered in the minds of the *Lost* crew and actors.

Even if the crew of *Lost* was able to write, film and produce enough episodes to fill all of the fall and spring halves of the typical television season with brand new episodes, the fans and critics would still find something to complain about. It is admirable that the producers and the network have tried so hard to appease the fans, but even they know it is impossible to please everyone. It is worth noting that *Lost* followed the same shooting and airing schedules in its first two seasons that every other show did during those seasons, with few exceptions. So why was there so much scrutiny, so many attempts to rearrange a schedule that was not substantially different from that of its peers?

Because *Lost* always leaves the fans wanting more. Because the show is so absorbing and connects so deeply with its audience that its absence is more notable. That is not such a horrible problem to have.

So *Lost* getting an end date is a good thing. It's what Damon Lindelof and Carlton Cuse and the rest of *Lost* Labs wanted. It will give the fans the resolution that they have waited so long for . . . and still may not be entirely pleased with, but at least they will get something. And something is always better than nothing. As James Poniewozik from *Time* magazine put it, ". . . it may just offer a way forward for TV. It may seem insane for ABC to leave money on the table by limiting *Lost* to six seasons. . . . In an era of smaller audiences, networks need programs that can monetize a devoted fan base. But that requires assuring the fans — as limiting *Lost*'s run has done — that they won't be jerked around forever. TV may be an excessive medium, but the brilliant, groundbreaking *Lost* may just show it that quality can be quantity."

Chapter 20

WHY *LOST*
IS IMPORTANT

WHETHER YOU ARE A FAN who extols the greatness of *Lost* to anyone you come across or you spend the days after a new episode airs camped out in the "Didn't Love It" episode reaction threads at The Fuselage, the show has become a part of your life . . . otherwise, why are you reading this book? In the "big picture," *Lost* may be not much more than a short tangent in your life that branches off for a few years after the new millennium, extends through the year 2010 and then drops off. For those more directly involved with the show, the impact has been much greater and more visible. Award show hardware graces their offices and their IMDb.com profiles are plumped up with impressive nominations and wins. The once unknown names of Josh Holloway and Evangeline Lilly are recognized worldwide now — their privacy decreased significantly in the process. The creative duo of Damon Lindelof and Carlton Cuse will have offers thrown at their feet and projects green-lighted with little to no sales pitch necessary for many years to come.

Once it is all over, when the season 6 finale airs in the spring of 2010 and sites like The Fuselage and Lost-TV.com have faded away, what will *Lost* leave with us, the fans? Is the impact of the show so jarringly significant that

181

it necessitates books such as this one picking it apart, analyzing the fandom it spawned, as well as the dozen or so other *Lost* books that examine the show episode by episode, philosopher by philosopher? Are pieces of the *Lost* set going to end up at the Smithsonian so that future generations can look upon it and be awed by the show's importance to the history of television and to society as a whole?

There is no real way to answer these questions at this point in time. We are too close to it to examine it properly; the show still has too many stories to tell before critics can truly assess *Lost*'s place in the annals of television history. Still, it is worth noting the short-term effects of the show, because that lays the groundwork for what we will say about *Lost* when we look back with 20/20 hindsight.

When asked what his proudest moment has been with *Lost* thus far, Bryan Burk was on the verge of being stumped for a reply. The question was one he had not been asked before, so it required some deliberation. The answer he ended up giving was not, as might be expected, the Emmy wins or any of the other awards. It had to do with how the show came about in the first place:

> It came very early on . . . You know when you think about it — it's hard for people to understand this . . . it's hard to understand that everything about this show — the odds were stacked against us. We didn't have a script. We didn't have actors. The [pilot] season had already started. There were nothing but strikes against this show . . . serialized dramas did not work. Shows with science fiction elements did not work. We were shooting far away . . . the guy who greenlit the show was fired in the middle of production . . . But the idea that we got to do a show and it's turning out to be what we always dreamed it would be is — I supposed that's the most rewarding thing . . . to have an idea and have everyone you are working with totally agree on what it should be, and to have a studio and a network let you do it. You know, when does that happen? . . . we all stuck to our original vision and it's worked.

The showrunners took a lot of risks to get this show on the air, and the odds were stacked against them. And yet, it did succeed and has continued to succeed, sometimes in spite of itself. Other networks and even ABC have tried to duplicate *Lost*'s success with similar programming, but nothing else has really caught on the way that *Lost* has. So there has to be *something* special about *Lost*, right? Something that maybe is not so easily definable.

As Burk says, one element of that certain "something" is the likemindedness of those individuals who have created this show and who bring it to us every week. J.J. Abrams' nepotism when it comes to staffing his television shows and movies is legendary, though most reporters tend to focus on when

>: "Okay. Yes. Jack in Thailand was not our finest hour. But wait 'til you see Matthew in the finale. Unbelievable. We are blessed with the most amazing actors in the galaxy."
— Damon Lindelof, 5/3/07

>: "Re: the question and answer cycle — well, that's what we do here at lost labs. Wouldn't be any fun if we just answered everything. Then what? 'tonight on lost — Hurley eats a coconut!'"
— Javier Grillo-Marxuach, 7/13/05

>: "Weird about that Whedon thing. I guess he never got the note. And do you know how long it took me, cutting out all those letters from newspaper advertisements? Oh well. Guess I'll just have to KEEP THOSE WRITERS. And Drew rarely listens anyway. One less ear shouldn't mean much."
— J.J. Abrams, 1/2/05

(All quotations from TheFuselage.com)

and where J.J.'s best friend and designated "lucky charm" — Greg Grunberg — is going to show up. But it reaches so much farther than that. He has a producing partner, Burk, that he trusts implicitly. He uses the same casting director — April Webster — for everything he does. He prefers to use the same special effects guru, Kevin Blank; the same composer, Michael Giacchino; the same production designer, Scott Chambliss; and so on. He typically likes to bring in writers and directors for his television shows who he has worked with before, and the same goes for his actors. This symbiosis with colleagues in the industry goes both ways — most of those actors, writers, directors, etc., who have worked with J.J. Abrams look forward to working with him again. Abrams is not a man who burns bridges in Hollywood. He keeps those he works best with close at hand, and he likes to promote from within. There are examples of assistants becoming producers, editors becoming directors, writer's assistants becoming writers. For anyone who has met J.J., whether they be in the industry or just a fan, he is completely engaging and generous, almost to a fault.

It is this atmosphere into which Damon Lindelof and Carlton Cuse were absorbed during that first season of *Lost*, and it is safe to say that they not only learned from the J.J. method of forming a tight-knit group of people to create a show, but they managed to morph it into their own clique of individuals with complementary talents and minds. There have been bumps and misfires along the way, but sitting here at the end of season 4, it is not much of a stretch to claim that the creative team for *Lost* shares an enormous amount of loyalty to the showrunners. There will always be talented writers and directors and actors out there, but it is sometimes better to choose the people who are the best fit, rather than those who may have the heftier or more impressive resume.

Another "something" that is important to consider when measuring *Lost*'s impact is how it has handled the fans of the show. *Lost* is not the first show to have people behind the scenes reach out and touch fans — the creators have just done a better and more widespread job of it than you see done for most other shows. The Fuselage alone transcends any other show's success at inter-acting with fandom, but it is not necessarily a formula for fan interaction that other shows can duplicate. It's not just that some writers, producers and actors have come online and answered questions about the show, its success lies in the venue that has been used and the types of people from behind the Hollywood curtain who are making the effort. Damon Lindelof has stated that it was not too long ago that he was on the other side of the computer screen, going to bul-letin boards for his favorite shows and just being a regular fan. The Fuselage is important because of the people who used that avenue in the beginning — and those who still go there today. If it weren't for people as tech savvy and brilliant as Damon, Javi, Burky, Jorge, etc., coming to the site and embracing it and the fans who post there, the impact would be minimal at best. But they did come there — and some still do.

One of the most important elements of The Fuselage was that it gave the creative team a venue to shoot down rumors and debunk myths. The depth of the plotlines in *Lost* plus the writers' fondness for Easter eggs and archaic references have made fans of the show very Internet dependant. It does not take much for someone's idle speculation to turn into an outrageous rumor within minutes of it hitting the web. With the level of complexity in the *Lost* story, the fandom could have easily become mired in rumors and outrageous theories that would cycle pointlessly through various fan sites. Thanks to The Fuselage, it was possible from the very beginning to get simple questions answered or rumors dismissed. The successful quelling of these fandom fires could be partly responsible for the decision by Damon, Carlton and ABC to start the official *Lost* podcasts. Suddenly, Damon and Carlton became the most accessible showrunners in the biz — and it didn't stop there.

There are few fans who can say that *Lost* has had a bigger impact on their lives than kyuss92 and dondant. They met at Destination: LA 2 and were married before LOST Weekend 2007 came around.

Damon Lindelof and Carlton Cuse quickly have become remarkably accessible to fans, and not just online or through iTunes, but by showing up at conventions and the *Lost* fan parties, as well. Damon in particular has sought out chances to meet fans face to face, never forgetting his own fandom roots. Though the two men have been known to show up individually at events, they usually prefer to make appearances and do interviews together known fondly as "Darlton" to the fans. They have gone to great lengths to put up a united front and make sure everyone knows who is running the show. Not only have they made attempts to quash rumors and seal up spoiler leaks, they have also come clean when certain things haven't worked, admitting to bad episodes and bad character choices.

All of this openness and reaching out to the fandom has led to a unique relationship between creators and fans. Lindelof and Cuse are not locked up in their studio offices, appearing only when they get nominated at award shows. They are at Comic Con; they are being interviewed by Michael Ausiello for *TV Guide*, Kristin Dos Santos for E!, Doc Jensen for *Entertainment Weekly*; they can be heard on podcasts and sometimes seen in video podcasts. Even during the writers' strike they were visible — Carlton as part of the negotiating team and Damon as a fixture on the picket line.

The drawback to all of this accessibility is the fact that some fans believe they control the destiny of *Lost* since they can practically reach out and touch the showrunners. Quite the contrary, Damon and Carlton have continually tightened their reins on the show as the seasons have progressed — and now that they have negotiated their deal to bring *Lost* to its desired conclusion in spring of 2010, the impact of fan opinion will probably lessen even further. But that's just it: they negotiated the end of *Lost* for the fans. *Lost* getting an end date is *not* a bad thing — it is for the good of the show and, by extension, the good of the fandom.

It is impossible to discuss the impact of *Lost* without mentioning some of the more innovative marketing that *Lost* took risks in developing. The first ARG, known as The Lost Experience, was a huge undertaking for the fans who pursued it like any other ARG, and yet the majority of the viewing audience probably had no clue that it took place, much less that it resulted in a second ARG, Find 815, and a third, Octagon Global Recruiting, which was launched in the summer of 2008. These were very specific and targeted campaigns, geared to ensnare the most hard-core of the *Lost* online fandom — and it has succeeded fairly well.

Other marketing strategies that came from outside the typical television marketing box included Apollo bars (which were connected to the first ARG and have made appearances in the show itself); billboards across the country and across the world (as part of the Find 815 ARG); a forgettable novel, *Bad Twin*, "written" by Gary Troup (aka the guy who got sucked into the engine in the pilot episode); some of the most infuriating puzzles ever issued, thanks to the lack of a full picture of what the completed puzzles would look like; weird commercials from the Hanso Foundation; and some ape named "Joop." When your show can claim one of the most intelligent fandoms in television, it appears you can try anything at least once. As fans began making efforts (and sometimes succeeding) to influence the Powers That Be with innovative marketing campaigns of their own, *Lost* found a way to bring fans deeper into the show by enlisting their own marketing strategies, something that most shows would not bother with at all.

For a while now, *Lost* has become a puppet with no strings — cut loose from convention and setting out to take risks. But increasingly, it seems that risk taking is *Lost*'s legacy. As fans of *Lost*, we have front row seats to a show that is like no other, and that has created this fandom like no other. Our gratification has been delayed, spread out over four seasons already, with two left to go. As agonizing as the wait can be, it so far has been so very, very worth it.

APPENDIX

Fandom Slang — A Dictionary

Authors' Note: This fandom slang dictionary is specifically for the *Lost* fandom. Some terms, abbreviations and acronyms have different meanings in different fandoms.

Admin(s)
Short for Administrator(s). Used in reference to the owners of an Internet bulletin board. The Admins occupy the highest level on the bulletin board food chain.

alias
The username a member chooses to use on an Internet bulletin board or anywhere else on the Internet that requires a login. Some people use their real name, but most use an alias. See also "handle." ("Alias" is also a great television show.)

ARG
Alternate reality game. ARGS have been around for a while, but have become more common in the present as online role-playing games (RPGS) that entail going to various websites, obtaining passwords and clues via the websites or game e-mails, all leading to the information needed to progress in the game and come to the eventual finish or

endgame. In relation to *Lost*, there have been three ARGS (so far): The Lost Experience, Find 815 and Octagon Global Recruiting.

avatar

An image or character created by a user to represent him- or herself. Avatars are either three-dimensional (as in a character created for a role-playing game) or two-dimensional (as in a picture created for a blog entry or other community interaction). Also known as icons.

Bencatraz

Nickname for the other island, or more appropriately "The Others' Island" on which Jack, Kate and Sawyer were held captive during the first part of season 3. Home of the Hydra Station. It is a combination of "Ben" (as in Benjamin Linus) and "Alcatraz" (as in the California island prison).

Benry/Fenry

Nickname for Benjamin Linus's character. When we first meet Michael Emerson's character, he says he is Henry Gale. We then discover that he is *not* the real Henry Gale, so he was referred to as "Fenry" — a combination of "fake" and "Henry." When his real name is revealed, the fandom took to calling him "Benry" — a combination of "Ben" and "Henry."

boar

The *Lost* fandom's version of a "troll." A boar/troll is someone who comes to an online bulletin board or blog and intentionally posts comments that are meant to enrage or push the buttons of the members or other commenters. Their intent is to rile everyone up then sit back and enjoy the carnage. See also "ONSer(s)."

Bowlapalooza

Name of the annual bowling competition between the Burky Babes (fan group for *Lost* executive producer Bryan Burk) and the javiminions (fan group for former *Lost* writer and supervising producer Javier Grillo-Marxuach), usually held in conjunction with the annual *Lost* fan party, LOST Weekend (formerly known as Destination: L.A.).

BTW

By the way.

bulletin board

An online message board or forum. Members join the board, then they can post topics or questions (much like putting a flyer up on a cork bulletin board in the office break room or the student lounge) and other members come in to comment on whatever the topic is or to answer the question. (See also "threaded board.")

Burky

Nickname of *Lost* executive producer Bryan Burk and the alias he uses when he posts on The Fuselage.

Darlton

Shorthand for the team of Damon Lindelof and Carlton Cuse.

Destination: L.A.

Name of the first two *Lost* fan parties held in California. The first party (aka DLA1) took place in Los Angeles in April 2005. The second party (aka DLA2) took place in Pasadena in May 2006. (See also "LOST Weekend.")

DLA/DLA1/DLA2

See "Destination: L.A."

Easter egg

In relation to *Lost*, anything that is more than what it seems to be within a frame of film, an episode or the show as a whole, and is intentionally put there by the creators.

fanart

Refers to the making of avatars/icons, wallpapers, video tributes, mood themes and manips for a particular television show, actor, movie, etc., that you are a fan of.

foiler

A fake "spoiler."

FTW

For the win.

Fuse, The

Nickname for The Fuselage.

Fuser(s)
Nickname for members of The Fuselage.

FWIW
For what it's worth.

gacked/ganked
Taken from someone or somewhere else; slang for "yanked."

glomp
A particularly forceful Internet version of a hug — the equivalent of you jumping on top of someone and "chomping" on them because you haven't seen them in a long time or you are just particularly happy to see them.

handle
The username a member chooses to use on an Internet bulletin board or anywhere else on the Internet that requires a login. Some people use their real name, but most use a handle. Taken from CB and ham radio users, who refer to each other by their "handles" rather than their real names. (See also "alias.")

Hater
Someone who "ships" Hurley with Kate. (See "shipper.")

IMHO
In my humble opinion. Used by posters and bloggers to label something they have said as being of their own opinion and not necessarily something anyone else would agree on.

ION
In other news.

Jacket
Someone who "ships" Jack with Juliet. (See "shipper.")

Jater
Someone who "ships" Jack with Kate. (See "shipper.")

jears
Short for "Jack's tears," which occur so frequently on *Lost* that the fandom bestowed an abbreviation on them.

Jesus Stick
Nickname for the engraved walking stick used by the character Mr. Eko.

Lage, The
Yet another nickname for The Fuselage.

Lager(s)
Yet another nickname for members of The Fuselage.

LB
Linear board.

linear board
Also called LB, an old-time scrolling board that resembles a continuous conversation and is not divided into separate topics the way a threaded board is.

lolcat
An image or screencap with a caption added, usually in some form of chatspeak or lolspeak (in other words, using bad grammar and spelling words out as they sound, not as they are actually spelled, e.g. "O RLY?" for "Oh really?"). "lol" is from "laugh(ing) out loud" and "cat" is because most of the early ones were done with cats. Also known as "macros."

Lostie(s)
The 48 survivors of Oceanic Flight 815 who were from the main section of the plane. In other words, our main characters on *Lost* and the other nameless characters we see in the background (for these characters, see "socks"). Some *Lost* fansites and media outlets also refer to *Lost* fans as Losties.

Lostkateer(s)
Nickname for fans of *Lost*, mainly the ones who post on The Fuselage. It is a combination of "Lost" and "Mousekateers" — an homage to fans of another show from Disney: *The Mickey Mouse Club.*

Lost Labs
Refers to the Writers' Room of *Lost*, but has come to be associated with any member of *Lost*'s creative team who is located in Los Angeles (as opposed to Hawaii). The phrase is also meant to distinguish the creative team from the powers that be at ABC/Touchstone/Disney (aka TPTB).

LOST Weekend
Name of the third and subsequent *Lost* fan parties held in California. The first LOST Weekend took place in March 2007. (See also "Destination: L.A.")

lurk/lurkers
To lurk is to go to a bulletin board or blog and not participate in the discussion, choosing instead to just sit and read, but not engage. A lurker is someone who makes a habit of this.

manip
Short for "manipulation." Refers to alterations made to photos or screen captures, manipulating them to depict something or someone other than what they originally depicted.

meatsock(s)
Those unnamed characters we seen in the background. (See "socks.")

moderator(s)
The equivalent of police for online bulletin boards/forums. Moderators (or "mods") keep the peace, dispensing warnings to posters who disobey the Site Rules, handing out points (the accumulation of which can lead to temporary or permanent banning from the site), etc. On The Fuselage there are three different levels of mods: Ultra-Moderators (UMods), Super-Moderators and Mini-Moderators. All Mods are outranked by the Admin(s).

NSN
New show night.

Nomad, The
Damon's alias on The Fuselage. "Nomad" is "Damon" spelled backwards.

n00b

Refers to someone who is new to a show's fandom and/or a particular online forum. Pronounced "newbie."

OMGWTFPOLARBEAR!

Oh my God what the f*** polar bear! Reaction of *Lost* fans when it was first learned that the animal that Sawyer shot in the pilot episode was a polar bear. Since then, it has morphed to include any jaw-dropping/brain exploding moment of the show. Sometimes the "POLARBEAR" portion is replaced by an element of the new surprising moment, like "OMGWTFSHARK!" or "OMGWTFWALT!"

ONSer(s)

Nickname for people who come to the LB of The Fuselage, mainly on new show nights, and post a huge rant-filled and unspoiler-fonted post, then disappear. ONS stands for "one night stand."

OP

Original poster. The person who originated a thread on an online forum/bulletin board.

OOC

Out of character. Mainly used in fanfiction as a criticism when the writer of a story depicts a character from the show in a way that is not "in character" or not typical of how the character is portrayed on the show.

OT

Off topic. A blatant way of telling someone you are conversing with via instant messaging or in an e-mail that you are about to talk about something that has nothing to do with whatever you are currently talking about.

OTP

One true pair. Mainly used amongst shippers to refer to the relationship pairing that they feel is the ultimate pairing — their one true pair. For example, a Jate shipper would say that "Jack and Kate are my OTP."

pod

An industry term for a grouping of episodes. Why "pod"? It is unclear. The closest possible derivative would be the definition of a "social group of cetaceans (whales, por-poises, dolphins, etc.)." The term came into the *Lost* vernacular when describing how season 3 would consist of "two pods": a six-episode pod, followed by an extended hiatus, then ending with a 16-episode pod.

PTB
Powers that be. Refers to the people in charge of making the decisions about a show from the network executive level. Also referred to as TPTB.

PWN/PWNS/PWND
To beat someone or something so badly that you OWN them. To embarrass your oppo-nent to the point of humiliation. Comes from the realm of gaming and hacking — the use of a "P" instead of "O" does not have a definitive point of origin and was probably originally just a typo.

RPG
Role-playing game. Participants take on the persona of one of the characters and inter-act with other RPGers as that character. Usually starts with a defined set of circumstances or a particular environment and branches out from there.

Sceve
Combination of "Scott" and "Steve" — two famously indistinguishable background characters who were part of the original 48 survivors on *Lost*. To explain the craziness, it is best to bring the explanation from their fan group on The Fuselage, S.O.S. (Scott or Steve): "On and off screen, Scott and Steve have been a running 'joke' in regards to *Lost*. Who is who? Well, after 'Scott who was really Steve but called Scott' was killed by the Others . . . we were left with 'Steve who is really Scott.'" Due to the confusion, they are usually referred to as either "Dead Sceve" or "Alive Sceve." It is a bit of a sore subject for Damon — when asked about the confusion on The Fuselage, his response was: "Don't get me started on the Scott/Steve issue. Seriously."

ship
Refers to favoring two characters being in a romantic or sexual relationship with each other, as opposed to anyone else. You may ship Jack with Kate or you may prefer the Jack and Juliet ship. (See also "shipper.")

shipper

Someone who favors or "ships" two characters being in a romantic or sexual relationship with each other. In the *Lost* fandom, the largest shipper groups are those who ship Jack with Kate (see "Jater") and those who ship Sawyer with Kate (see "Skater").

Skater

Someone who "ships" Sawyer with Kate. (See "shipper".)

slash

Designation for "ships" and fanfiction that includes couples of the same sex in romantic and/or sexual situations. Female with female is usually further identified as "femslash."

Smokey

Nickname for the smoke monster on *Lost*.

socks

The Losties and Tailies who are not part of the main cast. The background characters on *Lost* Island, who have been dubbed by Damon Lindelof "meat-filled socks." The team of "Darlton" have also referred to them as "sock puppets."

spoiler

Premature information about plot that can spoil a viewer's surprise or enjoyment of a TV show or movie.

spoilerholic

Someone who is addicted to "spoilers" for their favorite shows.

spoilerphobe

Someone who goes to extremes to avoid all "spoilers" for their favorite shows.

Tailie(s)

Survivors of Oceanic Flight 815 who were in the tail section of the plane when it crashed.

TB

Threaded board.

tent pole
An episode or plot element strong enough to hold up other, lesser elements or episodes and attract viewers to them.

threaded board
An online message board or forum that is separated into various "threads." Members join the board, then they can open new threads with topics or questions, and other members come in to comment on whatever the topic is or to answer the question. (See also "bulletin board.")

thread-jacking
When a thread on a fan forum is taken over by someone other than the original poster (aka OP).

TPTB
The powers that be. Refers to the people in charge of making the decisions about a show at a network executive level. Also referred to as PTB.

video drop
When a new video appears on YouTube or is released on a website, it is said to have "dropped." The same term is used for the release date of a new CD or DVD, e.g. "The new Geronimo Jackson album drops on April 8th."

VIP
Very important poster. Used on The Fuselage to identify members of the board who actually work on or for the television show *Lost*.

ZOMG!
An alternate version of the acronym "OMG!" (which stands for Oh My God!). The "Z" does not stand for anything. As with most Internet slang, it is unclear where this variation originated.

BIBLIOGRAPHY

abc.go.com/primetime/lost/.

Abrams, J.J. "The mystery box." TED.com. Online. Accessed January 30, 2008.

Ausiello, Michael. "Why Did *Lost* Kill Ana Lucia? Lindelof/Cuse Tell All." TVGuide.com. Online. Accessed March 9, 2008.

Bernstein, David. "Castaway." *Chicago Magazine*. August 2007.

BryanBurk.com.

Burk, Bryan. Interview with author Amy J. Johnston. Telephone. February 7, 2008.

Campbell, Joseph. *Myths to Live By*.

—. *The Hero with a Thousand Faces*.

—. *The Power of Myth*.

DarkUFO.blogspot.com.

"David Fury Quits 'Lost' TV Show." SciFi.com. www.whedon.info. Accessed December 31, 2007.

"Destination: LA 2005." Video recording by HiddenSky. April 2005.

en.wikipedia.org/wiki/Babylon_5.

en.wikipedia.org/wiki/Farscape.

EvilPuppetMasters.com.

Grillo-Marxuach, Javier. Interview with author Amy J. Johnston. Telephone.
     August 23, 2007.

IGN.com.

Jensen, Jeff. "'Lost': Fantasy Island." *Entertainment Weekly*. July 2007.

"J.J. Abrams: The Mystery Box." TED.com. February 2007.

J-J-Abrams.com.

Johnston, Amy J. "Exclusive Interview: William Mapother, from 'Lost.'"
     BuddyTV.com. Online. Accessed April 10, 2008.

Keveney, Bill. "'LOST,' which way will it go?" USAToday.com. Online.
     Accessed March 18, 2008.

Sledgeweb's Lost . . . stuff. Lost.cubit.net
Lachonis, Jon. "BuddyTV Interviews *Lost*'s Damon Lindelof and Carlton Cuse
     — and gets answers!" BuddyTV.com. March 7, 2007.

—. "Interview: Josh Holloway from *Lost*." BuddyTV.com. January 30, 2008.

—. "Michael Emerson from *Lost*." BuddyTV.com. January 16, 2008.

"Lost! HERC chats up the cast in Hawaii." AintItCoolNews.com. Online.
     Accessed March 1, 2008.

BIBLIOGRAPHY

Lostpedia.com.

Malcom, Shawna. "*Lost* Fans Dramatically Divided Over a Double Death." TVGuide.com. Online. Accessed March 9, 2008.

Mapother, William. Interview with author Amy J. Johnston. E-mail. September 24, 2007.

"Mission: 'Lost' in Star Wars — J.J. Abrams and Damon Lindelof." StarWars. com. May 2006.

Nations, Gregg. Interview with author Amy J. Johnston. E-mail. January 28, 2008.

—. Interview with author Amy J. Johnston. E-mail. March 12, 2008.

Poniewozik, James. "Less Lost is More." Time.com. Online. Accessed May 24, 2008.

TheFuselage.com.

TheTailsection.com

"They're Making It Up As They Go." *Rolling Stone Magazine*. October 6, 2005.

Watch With Kristin. "Is Claire Dead? Are They Really Time Traveling? *Lost*'s Bosses Speak!" Eonline.com. Online. Accessed May 15, 2008.

White, Cindy. "Executive producers Damon Lindelof and Carlton Cuse promise that they've found the plot twists that will bring *Lost*'s viewers back." www.scifi.com/sfw/interviews/sfw14769.html. Online. Accessed March 23, 2008.

Wyatt, Edward. "Finally, Lost finds its way." www.nst.com. Online. Accessed May 15, 2008.

PHOTO CREDITS